Freedom to Choose

Two Systems of Self-Regulation

Freedom to Choose
Two Systems of Self-Regulation

Jack Novick, M.A., Ph.D
Kerry Kelly Novick

IPBOOKS.net
International Psychoanalytic Books

Freedom to Choose: Two Systems of Self-Regulation
Copyright © 2016 by Jack Novick, M.A., Ph.D & Kerry Kelly Novick

International Psychoanalytic Books (IPBooks),
30-27 33rd Street, #3R
Astoria, NY 11102
Online at: www.IPBooks.net

Interior book design by Maureen Cutajar
www.gopublished.com

ISBN: 978-0-9980833-2-2

This book encompasses the whole time span of our shared professional work so far. And so we want to thank again the many teachers and psychoanalysts we have learned from, our colleagues around the world, and the patients and families who have shared their lives and experiences with us. We dedicate the book to our younger colleagues and students who will carry psychoanalysis into the future.

More Praise for Freedom to Choose

In this slim volume Jack and Kerry Novick distill their combined century of psychoanalytic experience and thought into a clearly-written, practical guide that will help therapists and patients to reduce their dependence upon repetitive, dead-end patterns of feeling, behavior, and thought. Their description of closed-system patterns of self-regulation strikes chords that go back to Wilhelm Reich's "character armor" – patterns of defense which, while initially adaptive, become constricting and costly. Their technical handling of the constant oscillation between open- and closed-system functioning hat is characteristic of psychoanalytic work recalls Siegfried Bernfeld's comparison of psychoanalysis to a conversation that is begun, then interrupted but later (with effort) renewed and deepened . . . until it is interrupted once again (and so on). Into this old wine the Novicks blend and integrate current findings from the biological, neurological, and social sciences; they then illustrate their theoretical perspective with clinical examples that provide useful guidance to therapists both new and experienced.

The Novicks bring an Eriksonian approach to the way they frame both (1) development across the life span and (2) the phases of treatment. They describe how each developmental phase is characterized by a specific challenge and how that challenge can be met with open-system or closed-system responses (or, as is usual, both). Their schematic approach to the tasks encountered by patient, therapist, and significant others as they traverse the therapeutic landscape from evaluation to post-termination will be particularly helpful to trainees; but it also will be of value to experienced therapists who wish to re-view their clinical work through a new lens.

This book has implications not just for clinical work but also for the psychoanalytic profession itself, a profession which sometimes has mired itself in closed-system functioning. The Novicks' approach expands the domain of psychoanalysis; it also broadens the tools available to those analysts and therapists who venture into new territories. It stands in stark contrast to the many currently popular approaches which focus on the description and elimination of symptoms, ignoring the human meanings which lie beneath them.

A careful reading of the Novicks' book will sensitize readers to the presence of closed-system patterns in themselves, their patients, and the world around them. The result? An enhanced freedom to choose.

Paul M. Brinich, PhD, Emeritus Professor, Departments of Psychology and Psychiatry, University of North Carolina at Chapel Hill, Faculty member, Psychoanalytic Center of the Carolinas, Past President, Association for Child Psychoanalysis

This outstanding book presents in a remarkably comprehensive and insightful manner the model conceptualized by Kerry and Jack Novick over the past fifty years. This model provides both a profoundly psychoanalytical understanding of the human development and an innovative methodology for the treatment of children, adolescents and adults.

The Novicks offer a major and extremely useful contribute for the analysts and the therapists ,who will appreciate their theoretical coherence and the clarity and richness of the case illustrations. Every chapter reflects a most sensitive approach, founded on a continuous collaboration and on the vital importance of maintaining or reestablishing the "freedom to choose".

Enrico de Vito, M.D., Psychoanalyst, Associazione per lo Studio dell'Adolescenza, Milano.

The Novicks' innovative two-system model of development and treatment represents a major advance in psychoanalytic theory and technique. Although their model has been extremely helpful to me both clinically and theoretically for a number of years, I found reading Freedom to Choose a most enriching experience which offered fresh insights and understanding of both my child and adult patients. Time and again I found myself immediately able to usefully apply what I had just read to my clinical work. Reading the Novicks' latest contribution has the potential to expand one's understanding of development and technique in significant ways. Thereby, one's clinical work can become more effective, and analytic therapy can be helpful to a broader range of patients, both children and adults. In addition, this model holds the promise of providing an integrative basis for a number of major analytic theories usually considered to be conflicting and for integrating psychoanalytic theory and technique with contemporary biological science including evolutionary theory and neurobiology.

William M. Singletary, MD, child and adult psychiatrist and psychoanalyst on the faculty of the Psychoanalytic Center of Philadelphia.

This book represents the culmination of fifty years of experience by two of the most creative thinkers in American psychoanalysis. In this exposition and expansion of their two systems model, the

Novicks bring together their groundbreaking work on sado-masochism with their creative approach to the integration of ego psychological and relational approaches to clinical work. Not content to prioritize the intrapsychic or the environment, their two systems of self-regulation highlight how early and later unfortunate environmental interactions become internalized and part of intrapsychic conflict. As a result, the sado-masochistic behaviors and personality traits of the closed-system must be analyzed with consideration of the defensive and other dynamic functions they serve. On the other hand, attention to the open-system allows the analyst to support and encourage the healthier aspects of the patient's mental functioning in ways that earlier generations of analysts would have dismissed as merely supportive or parameters. This book is going to become a staple for training psychoanalytic candidates and other mental health disciplines on how to think and work clinically in an integrative and clinically sensitive manner. It will move us beyond today's pluralism toward a model that utilizes all that our disparate schools are learning about mental functioning, pathogenesis, and therapeutic action.

Alan Sugarman, Ph.D., Training and Supervising Psychoanalyst, San Diego Psychoanalytic Center Clinical Professor of Psychiatry, University of California, San Diego

Foreword

Putting this book together entailed our going over and going through all our writings in certain topic areas for the past 50 years. That made us think about it all as a body, but also as a stream that turned out to have more coherence than we had even realized as it flowed. Since we are psychoanalysts, not only of others, but also of ourselves, we associated to Elisabeth Young-Bruehl's remark about 'theory being biography' and wondered if that applied to us.

Of course it did. One of us grew up during the Second World War, learning to spot the planes of the Fascist enemy, with the idea that exclusion, externalization and dictatorship were evil. One of us grew up watching friends and family members assailed by McCarthyism, passionately loyal to ideas of freedom, fairness and autonomy. Both of us were profoundly influenced by the ideas of individual liberty, free will, and choice.

When we wanted to become psychoanalysts, the same values came into play. American psychoanalysis in the 1960s was still mired in exclusionary practices and regulations. Neither of us could train in the USA. We were both interested in working with children and we found our separate ways to the Hampstead Clinic, Anna Freud's training center for child psychoanalysis in London, England. Luckily for us, this was an epicenter for psychoanalytic innovation, research, and a combination of clinical rigor and experimentation. We were set on a path to work at multiple levels, gathering data from our experience with our cases, required to write things up at frequent intervals, which taught us to formulate, and exposed to the finest international psychoanalytic thinkers, all of whom passed through Hampstead repeatedly over the years.

We worked to understand Freud's body of thinking. Quite apart from the theoretical content about psychology and mental functioning, there were intrinsic and implicit assumptions about the value of each individual, a profoundly democratic idea issuing from a person living in an autocratic imperium, who also had his own struggles to engage with about power and authority. But the ideas were there and made an impact. There were values to internalize from Freud's work and inspiration from the example of Anna Freud's lifelong attention to the needs of underserved and un-understood groups. Seeing every day during our training the women who had cared for the children flown from concentration camps to a safe haven and an endlessly understanding home at Bulldog's Bank offered us the measure of what analytic devotion entails.

Another aspect of our full-time, immersive training, which we were probably unaware of at the time, influenced us profoundly. Everything at Hampstead happened in groups. When we weren't seeing our patients, or attending supervision, seminars, or our own analyses, our days were spent in meetings. There was the Baby Group, the Concept Group, the Clinical Concept Group, the Diagnostic Group, the Nursery Group, the Index Group, the Borderline Group, and so on. That meant that we had to learn to listen to other points of view, to other ideas, to make a case for our own, to examine the logic and relevance of everything put forward. It was a collaborative endeavor.

Freud described the idea of the "analytic pact." This sounds nice and straightforward to modern ears, but it was actually revolutionary. The idea that a doctor, the ultimate authority figure with the knowledge of life and death, would engage in a partnership with patients was deeply radical. This continues as a tension in our field, so Freud's innovations still matter and cause ripples. But it primed us to think about the contrast between different models of relationship in treatment, as well as in life. This is the basis of our interest in the therapeutic alliance.

This collaboration carried over to our initial work together. We came to the shared endeavor primed by our backgrounds to demand of each other an equal relationship, a collaboration. We might say that what emerged very quickly was an open-system recognition of partnership, with each of us appreciating the real capacities of the other. We began working together in the middle 1960s and that has continued over 50 years of productive endeavor. Our own experience together primes us to be alert to manifestations of closed-system functioning.

This book represents a collation of ideas that have emerged in relation to different questions and different challenges. We have come to see that organizing principles can be applied for understanding, but also for action. And when there is an organizing idea, applications can be tried, tested and improved.

Thus, while this book describes a long culmination of thinking, it is also only an interim report, a work in progress. Our two-systems model is in constant evolution. It needs and will benefit from amendment, elaboration, adjustment to the realities of the developmental and clinical data that emerge from our daily work and that of other analysts and therapists, and from developments in allied fields. We look forward to the uses colleagues can make of this book for thinking, teaching, and clinical work, and to the changes ahead in understanding how individuals grow and flourish.

The book is organized into two parts, the first describing our ideas about how a two-systems model illuminates issues in development through the life cycle, the second summarizing technical ideas about addressing open- and closed-system manifestations through the phases of treatment. At the end we include an annotated bibliography of our writings relevant to the two-systems model, a list of "distinguishables" informed by two-systems thinking, and a reference list.

Please let us know how this book is useful to you and what ideas it sparks, what questions or disagreements it raises, and how you want to extend or apply the ideas. Contact us at kerrynovick@gmail.com.

Contents

Introduction

For over fifty years we have studied destructive and self-destructive sadomasochistic behavior in individuals, from failure-to-thrive infants to uncontrolled violence in children, to murder and suicide in adolescents and adults. In ordinary clinical work, all the patients we see present with some degree of sadomasochistic functioning, no matter what the diagnosis. Repetitive, resistant, self-defeating functioning, stalling or impasse in the clinical relationship – these form the arena for most analytic endeavors. In our writings on these topics, we have particularly highlighted traumatic origins, helplessness, overwhelming rage, the impact of preoedipal, oedipal, and post-oedipal pathology, terror of affects and excitement, tyrannical superego, and the constant danger of self-destruction.

In this book we hope to present in summary form the basic ideas that have emerged from this work. Rather than detail the arguments, rationales, and underpinnings here, we will direct the reader to those in various other, more extensive discussions. Here we will bring into one place statements and descriptions of how our model of two systems of self-regulation has worked for us to generate a fruitful perspective on development and clinical technique. Part I of the book will take us through developmental phases from pregnancy to old age. In Part II we will turn to descriptions of how our two-systems model can inform and enhance clinical technique in therapies of various kinds.

Our interest in these topics came first from our wish to understand the problems in treating especially difficult child and adolescent patients at the Anna Freud Centre (then the Hampstead Clinic) in the 1960's. Starting with our own, and then looking at over 100 indexed cases from colleagues to find the most problematic treatments, it became clear that each of those cases showed evidence of a beating fantasy. Through seeking to understand Freud's statement that the beating fantasy is the "essence of masochism,"[1] we undertook in 1969 a study of beating fantasies in children.[2] Our beating fantasy study traced the origins of this central psychological phenomenon and led to describing a sequence of organizing fantasies in development. We concluded that the beating fantasy can be a normal transitional component of postoedipal development in girls and may be quite common, serving, among others, the function of establishing the difference between receptivity and passivity.

In contrast to the girls with this transitory beating fantasy, we have found children and adults, male and female, with a "fixed beating fantasy," which is a relatively permanent, organizing part of the individual's psychosexual life; it occurs in the context of severe pathology with accompanying ego disturbances and problems of the self. This is a crucial difference, as our findings about the occurrence of beating fantasies in a normal and a pathological form, with such substantive differences between them, suggested that we consider the development of these phenomena in a different way. An even more important and problematic question was enfolded in

We define sadomasochism as the conscious or unconscious, active pursuit or infliction of psychic or physical pain, suffering, or humiliation in the service of adaptation, defense, and instinctual gratification at all developmental levels.

those issues – are sadism and masochism part of normal development and functioning?

Our interest moved from that point to an examination of sadism and masochism through the whole course of development. Very quickly our clinical experience and our researches made it clear that sadism and masochism always go together. Hence our consistent description of either as sadomasochism. We concluded that we could define sadomasochism as the conscious or unconscious, active pursuit or infliction of psychic or physical pain, suffering, or humiliation in the service of adaptation, defense, and instinctual gratification at all developmental levels.[3]

Increasingly we saw an intimate circular connection between sadomasochism and omnipotence. At each point in the development of sadomasochistic functioning we discerned an underlying omnipotent belief, and in turn the sadomasochistic behavior was felt to justify the persistence of the belief. The critical link was pain – pain is the affect which triggers the defense of omnipotence, pain is the magical means by which all wishes are gratified, and pain justifies the omnipotent hostility and revenge contained in the sadomasochistic cycle.[4]

SELF-REGULATION IS BASIC

There is a fundamental need for homeostasis and mastery, which in turn underlie a sense of self and self-esteem. Each individual needs to feel safe, that his world is predictable, that his experience is encompassable, that obstacles can be overcome, problems can be solved and conflicts resolved. From infancy on, individuals can feel pleasure when such conditions can be assumed. However, when faced with overwhelming experiences, whether they originate from internal or external events, all people throughout life must find some way to feel good.

Research over the past thirty years has converged on the importance of self-regulation as an overarching biopsychosocial function: "the growth of self-regulation is a cornerstone of early childhood development that cuts across all domains of behavior."[5] Our two-systems model represents an effort to describe various ways individuals can and do actively seek safety, security and a sense of mastery to create a platform for survival, development and functioning.

THE CENTRALITY OF DEVELOPMENT – SINGLE AND DUAL TRACK MODELS

Psychoanalysis is, above all, a developmental theory and a model of development that informs all therapeutic techniques either implicitly or directly. Freud said in 1913 that ".... from the very first psychoanalysis was directed towards tracing a developmental process."[6] But what kind of developmental process?

In a single-track model pathology is understood to be rooted in, and extended to describe, all early development. Adult pathology is explained as fixation, arrest, regression to, or persistence of what was normal in childhood. To put it the other way around, in this conceptualization, what was normal in childhood is pathological in adulthood. Adult normality is explained as a sublimation or compromise formation on the basis of infantile "perverse" impulses.[7] There seems to be a perennial pull in our field, both theoretically and clinically, for psychoanalysts to stress this unitary, single-track pathological continuum. This implies neglect of the individual's strengths, capacities, push toward progressive development, and use of the opportunities provided by reality experience, including that of the treatment situation and relationship.

Modern psychoanalysis, as well as most current general psychological and neuropsychological formulations, seems to seek explanations for the clinical phenomena of difficult patients and developmentally struggling children and adolescents in what we see as a derivative of the single-track theory. The underlying hypothesis rests on the idea of deficiency, with many new diagnostic categories created to bolster the conceptualization, for instance, borderline, bi-polar, pervasive developmental disorder, oppositional-defiant disorder, and so forth.

From Freud on, however, there are also many instances of psychoanalytic thinkers, as well as many in adjoining fields, who have maintained the utility of a dual-track model.[8] This alternative psychoanalytic tradition of a dual-track developmental model touches also on the debate about linear and non-linear development. In the emerging interdisciplinary science of developmental psychopathology, researchers draw on biological and philosophical ideas to look at two systems of epigenesis, an open system of behavioral and biological plasticity, and a closed system where the initial conditions inevitably determine the end state.[9] A dual-track model better fits our experiences in clinical treatment of sadomasochism and our observations of development in other settings, such as psychoanalytic preschools. Our formulations therefore assume an alternative line of development in which potential different solutions to conflict may be achieved throughout life.

TWO SYSTEMS OF SELF-REGULATION

From our clinical work on sadomasochism and the defensive omnipotent beliefs and fantasies that organize it we build on a dual-track foundation to postulate two systems of self-regulation and conflict resolution. One system is attuned to reality and characterized by joy, competence, and creativity. The other avoids reality and is characterized by sadomasochism, omnipotence, and stasis. In various writings we have delineated these alternative solutions to conflict as two systems of self-regulation that we have called "open" and "closed," respectively.[10]

When we describe two systems, the competent one open to inner and outer realities, the omnipotent one closed within self-perpetuating, sadomasochistic beliefs and fantasies, we are not referring to distinct psychic structures, such as id, ego, superego, or particular developmental stages, or distinct topographic dimensions of the conscious and unconscious regions of the mind, each with a different type of thought organization, such as primary and secondary process.[11] Rather we are referring to two modes of conflict resolution and self-regulation, each of which is a possible response to conflict at any point in development. Each response, whether organized on the basis of open-system functioning or closed-system functioning, represents the person's best effort to meet legitimate basic needs. Each phase of development contributes a strand to the formation of an open or closed system of conflict resolution and self-regulation, which in turn affects development in each subsequent phase, and operates through deferred action to revise the memory and meaning of earlier phases.[12]

OPEN SYSTEM

At any point in experience or development, starting at birth, we discern a possible response to helplessness in the face of internal or external overwhelming through a system of self-regulation that is competent and effective, based on mutually respectful, pleasurable relationships formed through realistic perceptions of the self and others, open to experience from inside and outside and thus generative of creativity in life and work. Most importantly, the open system concept makes a place in our theory for the inclusion of creativity, love, collaboration, hope, mutuality, and cooperation in life and in the treatment relationship.

Later in this book, we will detail various concepts that have proved useful in understanding and working with open-system phenomena. In the section on development, we will describe the "emotional muscles" that can be nurtured at each stage in children and parents.[13] This concept derives from psychoanalytic ideas of ego capacities, developmental lines, and general characteristics of the ego, and relates also to formulations of resilience and protective factors drawn from allied fields. In the section on technique at different phases of treatment, we will stress the interrelation of open-system functioning and the therapeutic alliance.

CLOSED SYSTEM

In a closed, omnipotent, sadomasochistic system of self-regulation the active search for pain and suffering has changed experiences of helplessness into a hostile defense. The organizing *belief* in this defense against traumatic helplessness is one of magical power to control the object. Everything the person does is directed toward control of others. At various times in life, the individual has convinced himself that this defense is effective; indeed, there may have been times when it served as the best or only available adaptation to inner and outer circumstances. When the omnipotent defense is consolidated as a solution to conflict over time, it comes to serve multiple functions and motives, which leads in part to its later intractability in treatment. We emphasize that closed-system functioning is not a deficiency or deficit; rather it is a solution.

As our ideas about the development and treatment of sadomasochism along with the conceptualization of two systems of self-regulation have evolved we have developed a view that departs from the classical psychoanalytic description of "normal infantile omnipotence."[14] We see omnipotence as a *quality* that can be attributed to wishes, thoughts or daydreams. As such it can be a harmlessly pleasurable element of play or creativity, as long as awareness of the distinction between real and pretend, between thought and action, is maintained. There can be an illusion of omnipotence accompanying childhood fantasies. It is only when such ideas are validated from the outside by external factors such as serious medical conditions, death or other accidents of fate, or psychological trauma stemming from parental inadequacy or pathology, that an illusion of omnipotence is converted into a *delusion*. It becomes a central belief, a subjective conviction of the reality and truth of a particular conscious or unconscious idea.[15] Omnipotent beliefs present as convictions or assumptions that organize an individual's thinking and actions.

Closed-system functioning is not a deficiency or a deficit. It is a solution.

7

In our work we have emphasized that we do not view omnipotent beliefs as an inevitable part of normal development, nor as equivalent to oceanic feelings, grandiosity, egocentrism, primary process, or primary narcissism. Omnipotent beliefs are created in response to reality failures in order to protect the person from physical or psychological trauma. We define omnipotence as a conscious or unconscious belief in magical power to transcend all the limitations of reality in order to control others, to hurt them, to force them to submit to one's desires, ultimately probably to force one's mother to be a "good enough," competent, protective, and loving parent.

I

Development

1

Two Systems and Development

W e work with the following assumptions about development:

- A developmental approach is a crucial dimension of understanding the complex, multi-faceted determinants of personality.
- The developmental approach is what differentiates psychoanalysis from many other psychological theories.
- A developmental approach assumes that all behavior has meaning and a history.
- Development can only take place in the context of relationships.
- A person's history encompasses generations, at the very least the parents and the beliefs and fantasies they bring to rearing their children. Cultural influences are transmitted through parents and other relationships and experiences in life.
- Each phase brings something unique to the mix, which may compensate for earlier difficulties or raise prior dormant issues to problematic intensity (Nachträglichkeit or deferred action).[16] Each phase influences and is influenced by each of the others.
- Each phase of development poses a primary challenge

11

that can be responded to in various ways, with closed- or open-system modes of self-regulation.

- With open-system functioning behavior evolves through phases in which current levels of psychological and biological development influence and are influenced by previous phases in a non-linear way.[17]
- Transformation is the main characteristic of this open-system epigenetic evolution, in which no one phase has more importance than any other and developmental transformations continue throughout the life span.[18]
- Closed-system functioning tends to have a more linear, determinative, predictive pattern.

Beyond the phase challenges there may be internal or external factors that can turn ordinary difficulties into traumata. Children faced with any of the myriad mischances of life may feel unable to manage without recourse to magical, omnipotent defenses against the helplessness and rage engendered by circumstances beyond their control or mastery. By deferred action a later event or the developmental conflicts of a later stage may raise the earlier experience to traumatic intensity, and evoke an omnipotent response.

Response to a trauma need not be based on an omnipotent defense. If a parent and child are helped to draw upon open-system, competent resources, trauma can be mastered. This helps explain the mystery of children developing well despite traumatic beginnings. We assume, however, that repeated use throughout development of an open system of conflict resolution, and hence of effective self-regulation, strengthens everyone's capacity to deal with difficult experiences in a realistic, adaptive way.

Whatever the clinician's stance regarding the idea of development in general, we hope that the descriptions of open- and closed-system responses to specific phase challenges that follow can provide developmental images that resonate in work with people of any age, thereby increasing the potential for empathic understanding.

2

Pregnancy

It is well known, although not well explained, that personality characteristics are transmitted across generations. A robust literature documents psychological factors in parents as crucial influences on how babies come to experience themselves and interact with the world and other people.[19] There are many aspects of mothers' and fathers' personalities that could be isolated for study. Here we are focusing on how responses to present

Personality charac-teristics are transmitted across generations.

or anticipated helplessness, real or imagined, underscore the role of parental fantasies and beliefs in the unfolding psychological development of the child. Anna Freud often quoted Augusta Bonnard's remark that the "psychic reality of the mother is the external reality of the child."[20] We would extend this to include maternal fantasies during pregnancy.

Fantasies during pregnancy are central to a mother's preparation for parenthood. Wishes for a healthy baby do not violate anything really known about the unborn baby and can relate to normal maintenance of the mother's self-esteem: she wants to feel like a healthy woman who can produce a healthy baby. Anxieties that the baby may not be healthy can relate to the mother's preparation for tolerating the anxiety involved in protecting her child from reality dangers.

This exposes the mother to her own vulnerabilities in the area of maintenance of her own feelings of safety; this necessary empathic identification with her child's vulnerability evokes either a constructive adaptive use of her ego capacities to protect herself and her child or recourse to omnipotent, closed-system solutions. We distinguish between open-system daydreams that enhance the self, and may include transient pleasurable omnipotent fantasies, for instance, of being the queen birthing the princess, and unrealistic omnipotent beliefs or assumptions that have as their ultimate goal the control of others. Usually the manifest content or storyline of the daydream, worry, or dream cannot immediately tell us which it is; the closed- or open-system role of the fantasy or belief may emerge in further exploration.

WORRY AS MAGICAL PROTECTOR

Mrs. A, five months pregnant, worried that something might be wrong with her baby, despite every evidence that her pregnancy was proceeding normally. She remained preoccupied with these thoughts, despite work in her treatment on the various associations and derivatives of her worries, and the reassurance of her obstetrician and friends that such anxieties were normal. A month before my vacation, when Mrs. A noted that there were only four weeks left, she did not proceed to explore this thought, but instead turned to fears about her baby's intactness.[21]

To illustrate the theoretical point, we will describe here the intrapsychic sequence as we came to understand it together. Of course the material did not emerge in such tidy order. Central to Mrs. A's character, as we had discerned throughout her treatment, was her omnipotent belief that she could control everything, especially the feelings and actions of others. Although she was potentially a very creative person, her self-esteem and feeling of safety were rooted in this conviction, instead of in her realistic capacities. Anything that threatened her sense of omnipotent control left her feeling exposed and vulnerable.

Whenever I took a vacation, Mrs. A felt helpless and her delusion of control was threatened. My independent action undermined her usual way of regulating her feelings and her self-esteem. She responded to her feeling of helplessness with a rage that felt all-powerful and unstoppable. She then worried that the other person would be damaged. The only way she could protect others was to worry constantly. This was not an unusual pattern, and we had worked on all the elements of guilty defense before. The new aspect at this point in the treatment was our specific focus on the magical, omnipotent elements in the sequence.

First was her feeling that anything less than total control of the other person left her without love and protection. To be safe, protected, and loved, she had to exert power over others. She restored her self-esteem and managed her

Closed-system solutions eventually cause other problems.

feelings through the conviction that her rage was so powerful that it was uncontainable and could truly hurt another person. The trademark of a closed-system solution, however, is that it eventually causes a further problem. Mrs. A had then to deal with the idea that she would destroy someone she loved. What recourse did she have to solve this problem?

We described earlier two distinct systems of self-regulation, one rooted in reality-based interactions with the world, the other dependent on magic. Mrs. A's personality was rooted in her characteristic use of the magical closed system, and so she chose again to turn to an omnipotent belief that she could control the effect of her rage by worrying. When I took this up, Mrs. A replied that she always felt that something terrible would happen if she didn't worry. The act of worrying was the magical method by which she protected others from her omnipotent aggression. The connection between angry, aggressive impulses and worrying is a familiar one to which we are adding the perception of the omnipotent element that she clung to in order to feel in control, safe from terrifying helplessness.

Mrs. A, like all women, was vulnerable in her pregnancy to the real helplessness of not being able to control completely the safety and intactness of the baby. In her case, she responded in her characteristically omnipotent way to her feeling of helplessness by constant worry. When we understood and elucidated the magical thinking in her analysis, she was able to accept the reality of what she could not control in her pregnancy and turn her energies to what she could really affect. She began to concentrate on her health, the baby's room, her childbirth exercises, enlistment of her husband and others for support, and her pleasurable daydreams about her baby.

This was her first experience in the treatment of the possibility of a healthy alternative to the closed, omnipotent system of self-regulation. Through the rest of her treatment she repeatedly reverted temporarily to closed-system solutions in the transference and other relationships. But her new relationship with her baby as an autonomous individual remained relatively free of omnipotent beliefs of magical control. Her increasing investment in her parenting function became an important fulcrum for change in Mrs. A's analysis and for her baby's healthy development.

OMNIPOTENCE OF THOUGHT CROSSING GENERATIONAL LINES

Mrs. B presented a manifestly similar worry in her sixth month of pregnancy. Whereas for Mrs. A, the worry represented a characteristic magical attempt to defend against her feelings of helplessness, in Mrs. B defensive omnipotent beliefs combined with externalization to produce a more ominous picture. Mrs. B had been denigrated and thwarted as a young woman, and had submitted to her father's decree that she not pursue higher education, but meet his needs by working as his secretary. Her alternating submission to and rage at men was a prominent feature of her analysis. When she became pregnant, she assumed her baby was male, and then began to worry that he would have defective genitals. Mrs. B gained some respite from her anxiety with interpretation of her death wishes and the various condensed elements of her identification with her baby, but she continued to worry.

After the birth of a healthy boy, whose genitals were intact, she shifted to a fear that his legs were somehow malformed. Whenever Mrs. B felt frustrated by me for any reason, her fear exacerbated, and, without mentioning it in treatment, she took her baby for numerous medical consultations that were intrusive and rendered the baby helpless. Only after this material came inadvertently into the analysis, because Mrs. B had to change an appointment, could I make sense of the whole sequence.

Mrs. B's compliance and lack of anger had been noteworthy throughout the treatment. It was clear that this meek presentation was part of her transference to me as her controlling father, whom she idealized, even while recounting the history of her thwarted ambitions. The rage that accompanied her helpless submission emerged mainly in her relationship with her infant son, on to whom she externalized the damaged, helpless aspects of her self, as she identified with her father. Thus she had recreated with her son the sadomasochistic relationship she had experienced with her father, and was re-experiencing in the transference.

Part of her sadomasochistic pathology was a defensive delusion of omnipotence. Mrs. B truly believed that she could control others by being either the masochistic, compliant little girl or the sadistic father. She organized all her relationships around this closed-system conviction. Mrs. A's omnipotent belief related only to the independent action of the other, as when she told me, "I can accept who you are, I just can't stand having no say in what you do." Mrs. B's closed-system ideas additionally rested on defensive externalization, which violated the real attributes and personality of the other.

Mrs. B saw everyone, including me and her baby, as either powerful controllers or helpless, damaged victims, even in the face of glaring reality contradiction, such as her son's repeated clean bill of health. Her fantasies and beliefs during pregnancy persisted into her son's infancy, resulting in imposed experiences of helplessness for him. This case exemplifies one of the ways the psychological ambiance and personality of the mother can create conditions for the possible development of pathological adaptations in the infant. A mother who is driven to use omnipotent, closed-system defenses against helplessness interferes with the child's engagement with reality and fosters a dependence on unrealistic beliefs for self-formation, self-protection, self-esteem and self-regulation. Indeed, Mrs. B's son did later develop a disturbance, characterized symptomatically by a feeling of defectiveness and low self-esteem, and entered treatment.

As we go through the life cycle, looking at closed- and open-system responses to the universal challenges of each developmental phase, we find in examining phenomena in pregnancy that omnipotent beliefs are almost always a defense against feelings of helplessness. With support, most mothers who opt for an omnipotent response to their actual helplessness can set it aside and shift their energies to the realities they can enjoy and control. Without support, or when the omnipotent defense is embedded in more severe pathology, the closed-system reaction may persist through the pregnancy and cross the generational barrier to have impact on the newborn child.

With support, most mothers can deal with helplessness by focus on what they can enjoy and control.

We have started with pregnancy because it is the beginning of the life cycle for the individual; the mother's psychic state during pregnancy affects the unfolding of the infant's early experience. What we can learn from an initial look at the role of omnipotent fantasies, illusions, delusions and beliefs during pregnancy is that the strand of defense against helplessness inevitably persists throughout development. Even in adulthood, when the closed-

The type of defense against helplessness invoked in pregnancy persists through development. system response has undergone changes through many layers of development, and the possibilities of open-system responses have been elaborated and structured, the most minor manifestations of omnipotent defense, such as "knock wood," or "Thank God," or "Gesundheit," contain the strand of helplessness.

More substantive resonances appear in overwhelming formless anxieties of unknown origin, sometimes referred to in contemporary psychoanalytic formulations as "unrepresented states."[22] Many child and adolescent patients present with intense anxiety states that can be traced back to their own mothers' panic during pregnancy and beyond. Then there is a clinical challenge to disentangle worries and defenses, sorting out what belongs with mothers and fathers, and what belongs with the patient.

PHASE CHALLENGE: Parental helplessness re physical changes, intactness and safety of baby

OPEN-SYSTEM RESPONSE: Finding areas of realistic effectiveness and support; conscious planning to avoid repetition of own infantile experience.

CLOSED-SYSTEM RESPONSE: Helplessness leads to fixed image of baby as controller, devourer, savior; transference to baby from old relationships; externalization of devalued/feared/wished-for aspects of self on to baby.

3

Infancy

A ll phases can be described from a variety of vantage points: in relation to the development of closed- and open-system functioning, the important dimension we highlight in infancy is the pleasure economy and its corruption. Ordinarily, a baby's real capacity to elicit the appropriate

Pleasure is the central organizer of experience in infancy.

response from the caregiver, to get her needs met, is the source of feelings of competence, effectance and reality-based self-esteem. The capacity of the parent-infant couple to repair inevitable breaches in their empathic tie is an equally important source of feelings of competence and positive self-regard. A range of positive feelings from contentment to joy becomes associated with these competent interactions and comes to instigate, reinforce and signify empathic interaction. Thus pleasure is dependent on and regulated by the capacity of each partner for realistic perception and interaction with the other, which leads in turn to the satisfying experience of having an actual effect on the other.

There can be outside interferences to the unfolding of this normal development, for instance, from harsh circumstances or medical problems, mild or severe, in either mother or child.

PREVENTION OF A PAINFUL
MOTHER-INFANT INTERACTION

Baby Alice was born with a moderate congenital malformation of the heart that required surgery within the first few months of her life. Her parents were very anxious; they found it difficult to minister to her ordinary needs for feeding, diapering, and soothing without worrying that they might endanger her. They thought that they could keep her safe if they didn't touch her. Their concern for her cardiac functioning had spread to fears about the rest of her body and her psychological intactness. They needed professional clinical support to help them distinguish the reality dangers, about which they were doing everything they could, but were helpless to amend, from their worries that could indeed jeopardize Alice's emotional development. This is the distinction between a closed-system response and an open-system engagement with the reality of the situation.

With the help of a child analyst, the neonatal nurse taught Alice's parents how to care for her up to and through her surgery. The emphasis was on their capacity to provide good experiences for her, so that her mother could begin to learn to read Alice's signals accurately and feel effective in meeting her needs and her father could support those efforts to create a strong positive bond.

From the side of the infant, the parents were helped to see the importance of giving Alice the maximum experience of pleasure from making her needs known and having them met, to offset the helplessness and pain consequent on the medical interventions. In this way, Alice laid down open-system foundations for feeling competent in her interactions and deriving pleasure from her own capacities. Alice's subsequent development was excellent.

If there is no support for the normal development of pleasure in competence, or there is pathology in the mother such as we referred to in the chapter on pregnancy, or there is painful experience in infancy such as we have reconstructed in the treatments of sadomasochistic patients, the infant is at risk for corruption and deformation of the pleasure economy. Instead of repeated and accumulating experiences of pleasure in getting needs attended to, the baby's inborn capacities to elicit needed responses are ineffectual. The infant's experience of cause and effect is then formed and formulated in relation to painful feelings.

If a mother does not smile in response to her baby's smile, but only on emergence from a depressed or anxious state, or at arbitrary times, the only constant for the baby in an unpredictable life will become frustration and the whole range of dysphoric feelings. Mothers become associated with pain, indeed, the currency of existence becomes pain, since bad feelings accompany every effort to have basic needs met. Pain is central to sadomasochistic pathology and is a trigger for the omnipotent defense, for a closed-system response to the developmental challenge, as the baby is helpless to effect change without the intervention of parents or caregivers attuned to his needs.

In later years, when closed-system functioning is entrenched at all levels of development, the central element of pain can be understood to hark back to infantile experience, to this early layer of the magical use of pain for safety, comfort, and control. The basic needs of attachment, good self-feeling, and predictability become connected with feelings of helplessness and pain to secure their gratification; what ought to be pleasurable is transformed into pain.

Pain then becomes the affect that triggers the defense of omnipotence, pain is the magical means by which all wishes can be gratified, and pain justifies the omnipotent hostility and revenge contained in omnipotent, sadomasochistic, closed-system beliefs. Because the baby's developing sense of power is not rooted in actual experiences of effectiveness, there is no reality to contradict his illusion of control through dysphoric feelings and to counteract the development of an encompassing delusion, that is, an omnipotent belief.

CORRUPTIONS OF THE PLEASURE ECONOMY

Videotaped interactions between "Tabitha" and her mother throughout her infancy illustrate constant disruptions of Tabitha's play. Instructed to "be with your baby" for a film at 6 months, Tabitha's mother put her down on the floor on her tummy and sat down next to her with a few rattles. Mother shakes the rattles, immediately engaging Tabitha's interest. Tabitha reaches for a rattle, but her mother keeps jingling it just out of her grasp. Soon Tabitha turns in frustration and reaches for her mother, who flinches away, saying "No" and redoubling the noisemaking with the toy. Tabitha keeps trying and the sequence repeats several times; her persistence in the face of such frustration is agonizing to the viewer. Each time she fails, she turns to her mother, who refuses contact. When Tabitha does grasp another toy, as her mother looks momentarily away, she immediately mouths it, only to have it pulled from her mouth and her hand by her mother. Eventually she crumples, whimpering in a high, pathetic voice. Then her mother gathers her into her arms, hugging and crooning. We discern in this film the habitual association in the child's experience of disruption of competent functioning and attachment with painful helplessness.[23]

In a videotape filmed as part of a regular developmental record, teenage mom "Kathy" and her 2-week-old daughter "Nicole" are seen enjoying a feeding, with the infant gazing into her mother's eyes. Not so long after, in a film of feeding at 2 ½ months, we see Nicole trying hard to engage her mother with her eyes and her facial expressions. Kathy's developmental level and the onset of depression inhibited her appropriate responsiveness; gradually Nicole's smiles changed to a habitual frown. Nicole's mother began to make clear her displeasure and disgust with the baby.

Observations recorded her attribution of failure to Nicole. Kathy externalized unacceptable aspects of herself onto the child. At 4 months Nicole was diagnosed failure-to-thrive, coincident with her mother's deepening depression. Nicole turned to self-comfort, in particular to hair-pulling, tweaking and twiddling her hair until it broke, just at the back top quarter of her head, on the side where her mother held her in the crook of her arm, in the only consistent contact between them during this period. For many months the spot was nearly bald, and it remained noticeably shorter and ragged there for several years. This symptom represented an early attachment via pain, the first strand in a sadomasochistic development, and a first closed-system attempt to control the object.

We will be looking at transformations throughout development of the child's involvement with pain, but what we are describing at this earliest level is a learned association. The clinical material of our sadomasochistic patients at later ages supports Stern's view, based on infant observation, that "it is the actual shape of interpersonal reality, specified by the interpersonal invariants that really exist, that helps determine the developmental course. Coping operations occur as reality-based adaptations."[24]

This is the foundation for the repetitive search for painful relationships, in which the person in later life seeks a magical, omnipotent way to restore early controls and meet legitimate needs. When we look for the early roots of closed-system functioning, we see that in infancy the pain of helplessness is changed into an affect associated with attachment, safety and control. Pain is transformed from a passive experience of helplessness into an illusory sign of safety, and eventually will be part of a closed-system, omnipotent delusion that gratification of these basic needs can be achieved only in a painful relationship.

Later resonances of this early experience echo in treatment for both patient and therapist. Patients may come to characterize their pervasive familiarity with painful, closed-system interactions in sensory terms, like the suicidal young woman who talked about the "smell of home." Analysts may have what we have called "developmental images" pop into their heads; this is an experience of or association to *a* baby, not necessarily yet a reconstruction of the history of this particular person, but rather a surfacing of empathic understanding about the kind of predicament facing an infant under adverse circumstances. The analyst may or may not choose to share the image with the patient – we will discuss such choices more fully in the technical chapters later in the book. Alternatively or additionally, a repeated feeling-state may emerge into the foreground of the analyst's consciousness insistently enough that it cannot be ignored, but must be tended to, with sharing in words or images. Thus interactions deriving from or rooted in infancy find their way into the therapeutic relationship and the attention of both patient and analyst.

During infancy, we suggest that a painful relationship, whatever the source, needs intervention to prevent the development of later pathology. In line with our epigenetic conceptualization of development, it is also important to think about what it means if a baby has to deal with potential or actual trauma in infancy and thus enters toddlerhood with closed-system solutions already part of his repertoire of defenses. A baby who has found relief, security and predictability in closed-system defensive responses to the ordinary or extraordinary challenges of his experience is more likely to opt for closed-system solutions when challenged in subsequent phases.

PHASE CHALLENGE: Infant's failure to evoke needed responses from important people.

OPEN-SYSTEM RESPONSE: Mismatch followed dependably by repair

CLOSED-SYSTEM RESPONSE: Traumatic overwhelming, helpless rage and frustration; turn away from reality and competence; reliance on magical controls; attachment through pain.

Symptoms may include failure-to-thrive, hair-pulling, head-banging, biting.

4

Toddlerhood

For most children toddlerhood is a time of exponential expansion of possibilities. The flowering of motor and cognitive capacities allows for rapid development and elaboration of competence in regulating tension states, feeding, dressing, and protecting oneself, and establishing bowel and bladder mastery. The normal developmental tasks, activities, and wishes of toddlerhood provide an opportunity to establish adaptive coping mechanisms, a sound sense of self accompanied by feelings of effectance, joy, and safety, a loving relationship to constant others, and an enormous expansion of ego control of motility and cognition. Parents' capacities to channel assertive impulses appropriately and "absorb aggression" are crucial to toddlers' growing confidence and pleasure in their new skills.[25] The toddler's libidinal investment in excretory functions and the associated sensations, and gratification in asserting wishes and effecting their satisfaction, are sources of both instinctual gratification and ego nurturance.

Seen from this perspective, toddlerhood is not intrinsically a time of sadism, nor of the rageful disruption of "normal omnipotence," as formulated in many psychoanalytic models of development. We see splitting, projection, projective identification, and defensive externalization as closed-system defenses, not necessary and usual elements of this developmental phase. When we attempt to distinguish normal

Toddlerhood is not intrinsically a time of sadism, nor of the rageful disruption of "normal omnipotence."

toddler development from pathological, either during toddlerhood itself, or in the derivatives apparent in the treatment of older patients, we look for the antecedents in this phase of reactions to experiences of helplessness. Accidents of fate, like illness or bereavement, may inflict helplessness and pain on a child. When these appear in a history, the question is the patient's choice of solution, and his environment's provision of possibilities. Has he chosen an omnipotent solution, that is, generated a closed-system response? Or has he been able to achieve an open-system response, a realistic adaptation to adversity? What are the roots in toddlerhood of such a choice?

Visible, active assertion of toddler needs and wishes produces strong feelings of the pleasure associated with effectiveness. When this is blocked, frustration and anger swiftly follow and amplify all other affects. This still does not constitute sadism. The permutation of assertion to aggression to sadism depends on what happens next. In our view the crucial shift occurs when the child feels helpless to deal with the internal experience of anger *and* the outside world offers inappropriate or inadequate assistance. When adaptive solutions are unavailable the child turns to omnipotence, the additional quality that changes aggressive and assertive impulses into sadism. Internal changes have taken place in the child; this is evident when they become the aggressors and initiators of sado-masochistic interactions with others.

Children turn to omnipotence when adaptive solutions are unavailable.

Thus problems in the toddler period do not usually arise spontaneously, because of the "terrible twos." And the solution is not to wait for the child to outgrow them. Sadism is created in the context of a sadomasochistic relationship. If mother and father are not sadomasochistic, assertion will be appreciated and enjoyed, aggression will be absorbed and channeled and resolution of mixed feelings promoted. We have not seen spontaneously-arising sadism in very young children in either our observational research or our clinical and educational experience.

The toddler stage is crucial in determining the quality of assertive and aggressive impulses and in fixing the pattern of dealing with them. It becomes easier during toddlerhood to see the mutual interaction and intergenerational impact of parents' and children's personalities. Emotions and our reactions to them are the major currency of exchange between parents and very young children, much more pervasive and powerful than ideas.

Everyone has to find a way to deal with feelings that can be experienced as too intense or overwhelming to handle. Our work on defenses demonstrates that parental defenses are often reproduced in their children's functioning.[26] Closed-system solutions for the adults are often reflected in closed-system responses in toddlers. The defensive aspect of the underlying sadomasochism of a toddler's closed-system functioning follows upon and reinforces the child's prior submission to a threatening environment. What was initially an acceptance of a parent's externalizations (messy, dependent, aggressive) in the service of retaining an emotional connection becomes an active internalization used by the child to maintain a needed internal image of a loving, protective, perfect parent, safe from the destructive rage of his aggression. From the point of view of defense, the closed-system, omnipotent, sadomasochistic behavior can be seen as an attempt to defend against destructive wishes from each level of development, directed against the mother,[27] utilizing the mechanisms of denial, displacement, internalization, and, via the internalization, turning of aggression against one's own body.

Closed-system functioning in toddlers often occurs when normal toddler impulses toward autonomy and independent functioning are experienced/defined as aggression by both parent and child. The struggle for autonomy first takes place in the realm of bodily activity; parents of children who show developmental

Toddlers can respond with closed-system solutions when normal assertion and autonomy are defined by adults as aggressive.

disturbances in this phase usually oppose independence and react to normal assertion as attack. These children lose the battle for autonomy and feel that their mothers or fathers only need and want them to be helpless, messy, incapable, dependent people. The parents and children become locked in an intense relationship experienced by the child as one in which each partner desperately needs the other for both survival and gratification.

Frustration of normal assertion may occur when medical interventions include periods of isolation, inactivity and pain for a child. In a toddler's mind parents are the source of everything good or bad; medical events are often experienced as punishments. Anxiety at such times can make parents less available as auxiliary egos to support children and defuse the traumatic potential of helplessness.

ASSERTION BECOMES AGGRESSION

We can see in films of play taken at intervals through her toddlerhood how Nicole's normal exploratory impulses, curiosity and creativity in her play were continually blocked and thwarted, leaving her helpless to predict what would happen next. In a film where Nicole, newly toddling, is retrieving a ball tossed by her mother from the home base of a blanket spread on the grass, we see Nicole enjoying the game. After several repetitions, Nicole starts to sit down on the blanket, reaching to hold the ball in her lap. Her mother protests, grabs the ball to throw it out of frame, and forcefully stands Nicole up to insist on continuing the same play. After Nicole again attempts to sit down with the ball, her mother once more tosses it away, but this time, while the child is fetching the ball, her mother gathers up the blanket, leaving Nicole no home base. Nicole circles in bewilderment, puts her fingers in her mouth, finally finds the corner of the blanket, which she snuggles, and then her mother repeats the whole sequence, with the result that Nicole's confusion escalates, her behavior pattern becomes more disrupted, and she finishes by twirling her broken hair around her fingers and sucking them in a regressive withdrawal. Without help from her mother, indeed with her mother the source of the interference with experiences of realistic cause and effect, proportional stimulus and response, and accurate learning of meaning in the results of her actions, Nicole retreated first to aversive isolation. Eventually she turned to sadistic control of her mother in the next few months, when she would laughingly defy even safety limits. A closed-system pattern of relating was set in motion.[28]

In our work with sadomasochistic patients, it has become clear that they entered the toddler period with little confidence in their own capacities, and further opportunities for competent interaction were blocked and frustrated. Assertions were experienced and labeled by parents as aggressive; channels for appropriate discharge were not made available, so the frustrated child did indeed become aggressive. Attempts at effective steps toward self-reliance were experienced by their mothers as stubborn battles for control; through externalization and physical intrusiveness the children were never allowed to be in charge of and own their bodies. Aversive or angry responses to mother's lack of empathy occasioned increasing spirals of rage, guilt, and blame so that the patients as toddlers had been made to feel responsible for their mothers' pain, anger, helplessness, and inadequacy. The continuing failure of the caretaking person to meet the child's appropriate need for competent interactions created a feeling of intense helpless rage that was defended against by omnipotent fantasies of control, rescue, and potential destructiveness.

The development of closed-system functioning in the toddler period is fueled by helplessness engendered by repeated blocking of pleasurable experiences of competence and by the development of greater specificity in interpersonal relations, leading to the transformation of generalized frustration into directed rage. But we must also explain the development of the fixed quality of omnipotent beliefs, the later delusional conviction, apparent in the functioning of patients of all ages who suffer this pathology, that they can *really* destroy another.

To the infantile strand of the transformation of helplessness into the closed-system control of attachment through pain the toddler period can add the strands of person-directed rage and the reality base for the later delusional conviction of the power of feelings for hostile omnipotent control of others. We think the conviction derives from the external confirmation of the notion that anger really is destructively powerful and can overwhelm, damage, or kill the parent. The child's functioning is responded to as omnipotently destructive or omnipotently reparative: through externalization of responsibility the child is told, "You're killing me, you'll be the death of me," or "Mommy has a headache, be a good boy and mommy will feel better." The child searching for a solution to his helplessness is offered the idea that mother's feelings and well-being depend on the child. The wish to feel effective is granted in the illusory form of the message from the arbiter of reality, the parent, that his anger and aggressive behavior is the best way to have his wishes fulfilled.

The belief that autonomy and assertion are destructive is often part of the mother's omnipotent belief system. There are mothers who threaten separation as a punishment, lose their children in department stores or the supermarket, return to work as a retaliation for feeling left by the newly-walking toddler. When parents lose their connection to their child or can only connect intermittently, children internalize this pattern and relate to themselves and others in an inconstant way. This may appear in treatment in a confusing unstable pattern of being with the therapist, in an unpredictably fluctuating sense of connection. The stage is set in toddlerhood for the development of a full-blown sadomasochistic relationship with the quality of omnipotence an essential component of the child's narcissistic economy; already self-regulation and self-esteem depend on proving the power to control the others.[29]

In our book on emotional muscle[30] we talk about "making feelings just the right size" and "tolerating mixed feelings" as important muscles that toddlers can begin to develop. It is an ordinary open-system task of this phase for parents to help their children master feelings, to regulate experience so as not to be overwhelmed, and to develop ways to handle what arises. Note that we have described above the way in which closed-system functioning promotes the invoking of closed-system defenses. We think that the concept of defense and the techniques of defense analysis that are needed to address and change a person's dynamic habits belong in that borderland of the closed system. In contrast, the realistic foundation of open-system functioning conduces to the development of adaptive coping mechanisms, what we have have called "emotional muscles."[31] In everyday settings, we talk to parents about the muscles they need to develop to do that work. It's important to note that we don't normalize temper tantrums and meltdowns, but rather focus on those moments as opportunities to help their children develop the capacity to modulate feelings.

EMOTIONAL STATES TO EMOTIONAL SIGNALS

In a preschool parent group Mariana's mother Zita described her growing puzzlement over Mariana's continued tantrums. She always made her daughter sit on a certain step for 3 minutes when she had a tantrum, but it didn't seem to make any difference. Zita said, "She's about to be 2 and I don't feel I have the right tools to deal with this." All the parents in the toddler group wanted to know how to handle a "meltdown," the times when their children became overwhelmed by their feelings. This usually referred to anger but it could be sadness or any upset. The main strategy parents had was "time out," sending the children to another room until they could stop.

In discussion the group came to the idea that, as upsetting as the meltdown was to the adults, Mariana and the other children were not intentionally being bad. The children were overwhelmed and helpless to handle their feelings alone; they needed a grown up to help them master the emotions, in a "*time with.*" Zita could stay with Mariana and talk to her about her feeling getting "too big" for her to feel in charge. She could sit with the child and help Mariana use her own strong muscles to make the feeling "just right" to hold in one hand – then they could look at it together and figure out what to do.

The parents understood that the aim is to master the feeling and turn an overwhelming state into a useful signal. In this context the family consultant could introduce the idea of "emotional muscles," analogous to the physical muscles the children were rapidly developing.[32]

This is the open-system alternative to developing sadomasochistic defenses. Equipped with dependable tools to manage feelings, or accept help in self-regulating when needed, toddlers can move into the next phase of development with a sense of agency and security.

PHASE CHALLENGE: Exploration and assertion frustrated.

OPEN-SYSTEM RESPONSE: Child's aggression is absorbed in constancy of parental love; exploration and assertion enjoyed; autonomy and independence a source of pride, with attachment strengthened at new level.

CLOSED-SYSTEM RESPONSE: wishes given stamp of reality – assertion becomes aggression becomes sadism; self-esteem derived from control of others; externalization by parents; identification with externalizing defenses of parents.

Symptoms include rages, sleep disturbances, separation problems, attacking other children, interference with development of speech, toilet mastery, bodily control, mastery of feelings (tantrums, inconsolability).

5

Preschool

Preschoolers' dawning awareness that there are mysterious parental activities from which they are excluded and for which they are not equipped is a blow to the dignity and self-esteem of all children. But those children who enter the preschool years with positive self-regard based on earlier feelings of competence from effective interactions with their real internal and external worlds are not devastated by oedipal disappointment. They have moved beyond possessive clinging to one or the other parent and are capable of pleasurable interactions with both parents, other adults, siblings and peers. They enjoy and take pride in physical and cognitive activities, have begun imaginative play and can happily amuse themselves for considerable periods of time. Their capacity to transform and set aside infantile wishes creates an internal distinction between repudiated baby wishes of the past and the more grownup, current- and future-oriented wishes of the nursery child, i.e., they attain a sense of growth over time, a sense that they are on what Anna Freud described as a path of progressive development. With such a feeling children can begin to delay, defer and accept the notion that they will find their own person to love in a grownup way in the future.

To foster such an open-system passage through the phallic-oedipal phase, parents must protect the child from excessive stimulation, set appropriate limits and impart sexual information at a time and in a form which the child can assimilate. The loving respect parents have for the child and for each other helps to modify the aggressive infantile sexual theories all children create out of their own bodily experiences. So, for children already responding primarily with open-system functioning to developmental and life challenges, whose parents function similarly, the inevitability of oedipal failure, though somewhat painful, will not be traumatic, but also both a relief and a spur toward continued developmental progress in realistic domains.

Children already used to closed-system responses, and children whose parents use predominantly externalizing defenses and organize their personalities according to omnipotent beliefs – they are likely to take a different route through the potential shoals of the preschool years. In our 1987 developmental delineation of the epigenesis of masochism, we said that a crucial transformation occurs during the phallic-oedipal phase, when the painful experiences in the earlier parent-child interaction become libidinized and represent for the child participation in parental intercourse. To the powerful motives for sadomasochism of the earlier phases is added the circumvention of the normal oedipal exclusion.[33]

In a later paper on masochism and omnipotence we noted that, in our sample of sadomasochistic patients, the oedipal period presented them with realities they could not integrate, realities that carried potential traumatic impact.[34] In classical psychoanalytic libido theory, the phallic-oedipal phase relates to a shift of libido from oral and anal zones to the phallic. There is a concomitant shift in relationships from a dyadic to a triadic constellation. An important distinction, sometimes overlooked, is that between phallic assertion and phallic sadism, which is not a necessary part of normal development.

Now we characterize those differences in terms of open-system, progressive and realistic flowering of capacities to express and pursue wishes, in contrast with closed-system maintenance of hostile, omnipotent interactions with important people in a child's life. Difficulties in including all three people in the loving milieu become part of a closed-system response to the challenges of this phase. Children's assessment of their impulses depends on parents' reactions; they define the accepta- bility and nature of wishes, and will contribute to the self-assessment that is internalized in the superego

Omnipotent beliefs persist when they are validated from the outside.

toward the end of this phase. Omnipotent beliefs and closed-system functioning cannot be maintained unless they are also validated from the outside; thus parental functioning is a crucial contributor to the experience and resulting personality structures of these years.

The contrast between open- and closed-system functioning can be marked on many dimensions. Joy is an expression of self-esteem that springs from inside, a self-confidence and unselfconsciousness that comes with safe, unconditional appreciation of the child's real self and capacities. The open system of self-regulation, including its contribution to children's good feeling about themselves, is grounded in reality. Manic excitement, on the other hand, relates to pathological, distorted narcissism, in which self-esteem is vested in unstable outside sources; it represents also an omnipotent compensation for humiliation.

Children who are laughed at, teased, or shamed have their self-respect attacked, feel helpless in the face of hostility from powerful adults, and turn to unrealistic solutions. The connection of humiliation with aggression at this level has profound implications: instead of experiencing oedipal defeat as legitimate frustration of libidinal wishes, which actually meshes with physical realities, the child may equate the humiliation with annihilation, obliteration, emptiness, and complete helplessness. This will affect all later situations that demand taking a risk; all later libidinal impulses can trigger this reaction and include these deep anxieties, creating ever more powerful motives for massive defense. If parents respond to exuberance as if it is hostile or really competitive, children begin to experience their own enjoyment as sadistic. They can no longer take pleasure in their own achievements without seeking further gratification in triumph over the other. This sets a pattern of closed-system sadomasochistic relationships with the self and others.

Such a pathological resolution of the Oedipus complex leads to two outcomes in relation to closed-system self-regulation. First, omnipotent, closed-system ideas are reinforced as an apparently viable solution to conflict. Second, there is no genuine resolution of the challenges of the Oedipus complex and thus no realistic internalization and consolidation of the superego. The child is constrained to return to closed-system mechanisms as a control and a regulator of thoughts and actions. He does not move beyond his parents as the center of his world, and so will have difficulty turning to new people in a genuine way later. And, without a viable conscience, achievements and accomplishments cannot be used as occasions for praise of the self, for satisfaction mediated internally.

The two-systems description of development at this level leads us to consider the issue of narcissism. Just as we suggest that everyone needs to find a way to feel safe, we assume that everyone needs to find a way to feel good about themself. Self-esteem is an essential catalyst in psychological functioning. But it can be grounded in an unrealistic image of self and others idealized or denigrated in a sadomasochistic interaction, what we could characterize as closed-system narcissism. Or self-regard can be rooted in an experience of pleasure in mastery of real, age-appropriate challenges, leading to open-system aspiration and striving.

PHASE CHALLENGE: Reality of gender and generational differences (Exclusion from adult activities)

OPEN-SYSTEM RESPONSE: Turn to reality gratifications, internal sources of self-esteem; development of autonomous conscience with both affirming and prohibiting characteristics, open to reality corrections.

<u>Signs</u> include curiosity in service of growing reality sense, development of independent friendships, capacity to use adults as resources.

CLOSED-SYSTEM RESPONSE: Child responds to trauma from overwhelming experiences (primal scene, frightening films, TV etc) by sexualization, denial and externalization; parental collusion with child's wishes promotes formation of omnipotent delusion; sadomasochistic fantasies and beliefs organize conscience, which is tyrannical, divorced from reality, unmodified by experience.

<u>Symptoms</u> include persistence of earlier problems, inability to give up transitional object, bossiness and controlling behavior, provoking attack, obsessional rituals, bedwetting, ego constriction.

6

School Age

The complexity of development in the school years has been understated in classical theoretical descriptions; similarly, the significant contributions of this phase of development to later functioning have been undervalued.[35] This also applies to an understanding of the closed- and open-system options available to the school-aged child and his parents. Hostile defensive closed-system functioning in latency is built upon the foundation of pathological earlier developments from preoedipal and oedipal phases, but there are crucial elements added in this phase. It is in latency that many characteristics of closed-system self-regulation are consolidated, with methods and structures becoming more fixed.

We have found a point of entry into closed-system phenomena in problems of treating sadomasochistic patients. There is a particular interest in relation to the school years, as the sadomasochistic patients we have studied had little open-system space to consolidate ego development and few realistic sources of self-esteem that could be internalized in a kind, adaptive internal conscience. For these children, the gap they experienced and tried to repair was not between the real and the ideal self but between the real and the ideal mother-child relationship. Defensive efforts, wishful fantasies, and omnipotent beliefs were aimed not at enhancing the real capacities of the self but at denying and transforming the pain and inadequacy of the parent-child relationship.

Unable to make use of real capacities to elicit appropriate responses from parents, these children fell back on omnipotent beliefs in sadomasochistic control of others to regulate their feelings and maintain their self-esteem. When there seem to be few realistic and dependable sources of genuine self-esteem, schoolchildren can create a vicious, self-reinforcing, negative circle. They feel shame and humiliation from victimization, which then justifies sadistic attacks on others or internally on the self, and this then leads to further shame, guilt, and humiliation, and wishes for revenge.

Closed-system functioning creates a static vicious cycle.

Closed-system functioning in latency demands immediate effects, with no work; indeed, beliefs in this domain always partake of magical means of implementation. Their goal is to change the other, not the self. The magic of thought, word, and deed is felt to be all-powerful and comes to be invested with all the force of idealization developed in earlier phases. As long as the magical beliefs remain internal, secret means of mental control, they are untroublesome to the environment and so may often go unchallenged, but persist underground, with reality-testing distorted more and more in the search for confirmation. This internal dynamic often meets with the adults' wishes to deny the seriousness of the situation and hope that the child will outgrow the difficulties. The major loss is the child's pleasure in his real accomplishments, which would offer fuel for open-system autonomous motivation.

Closed-system functioning aims to change others, not the self.

Usually, however, closed-system beliefs bring with them further anxieties. When they spill over into life and relationships, children in the school years are often given medication to control their worrying or the restlessness that may result from it. Medication only compounds the problem, as it confirms to children their damage and their helplessness to grapple with difficulties. It reinforces the notion of a magical solution, external to the child. There is also a tremendous secondary gain, in that the child's anxiety, fears, or phobic symptoms really do become a means of controlling the others in the family. Thus a loop is established, in which a child's painful experience again is felt, with reality confirmation, to be a means to control others and force compliance with omnipotent wishes.

This experience of feelings as overwhelming to the self and as a means to overwhelm others is a consequence of the bypassing of normal oedipal resolution. Without a consolidated open-system superego for dependable internal control, emotions do not develop their appropriate signal function, but are defended against with accumulating anxiety. We suggest that an affective sequence begins to develop in toddlerhood, as the little child thinks about causality and effectance, and continues to be elaborated in later phases, differentiating clearly in the school years. In children developing predominantly open-system functioning, doing something wrong triggers a signal of shame, then remorse, then the impulse to reparation. For children already feeling omnipotently and unrealistically responsible for things beyond their capacities, wrongdoing produces total humiliation over the reality of childhood helplessness followed by omnipotent rage and then overwhelming guilt, followed by externalization of blame or fantasies of revenge – anything to get the feeling of helplessness outside the self. Then the vicious circle is set in motion. Regret arises later in this sequence, with its implication of the omnipotent capacity to deny the reality of time and go back to undo the original fault.

This is the age when an open-system conscience can be consolidated and reinforced from inside and outside. General open-system functioning, that rests on recognition and respect of the individuality and separateness of others and the self, is bolstered by the pleasure schoolchildren can achieve from playing by the rules, expanding their competencies, forging empathic friendships with peers, and gaining approval from teachers and other important adults. There is a mutually enhancing relationship between ego and superego possible at this phase, as ego ideal and superego guidelines

Open-system functioning creates a self-reinforcing positive cycle of good feelings.

and strictures keep the self secure and allow room for safe, new experiences. Inevitable failures and limitations can be experienced as challenges demanding further practice and effort. The pleasure obtained includes a good feeling about attaining ideals and gaining approval from oneself and others, which in turn motivates the schoolchild to continue to live by the rules. Open-system functioning allows for continuing expansion of the personality with ongoing integration of the conscience into the self-representation.

A closed-system superego comes under attack during the school years from the progress of peers to functioning organized according to generally agreed-upon standards. Disparities in personality development among different children begin to be more evident in the early school years.

By this time, a closed-system superego is a crucial dynamic element in maintenance of closed-system functioning, as it supports, validates, reinforces and legitimizes the vicious sadomasochistic cycle that appears in the symptomatology summarized below. Such a superego begins by the school years to define the sort of person the child is – a bully, a victim, or a loner, and so forth. This necessitates further ego distortion and often involves the child in isolative manoeuvres or the development of a double life, with secret omnipotent gratifications masked by compliant behavior. This is another developmental choice point, where the child, usually with help, can transform a closed-system superego into an open-system structure, or consolidates the omnipotent, sadomasochistic superego.

We suggest that the propensity to seek closed-system solutions, based on omnipotent beliefs rather than realistic ones, can become fixed under stress in the school years and undermine later possible choices of alternative solutions. The multiple motives for maintaining the quality of omnipotence in mental life and the functioning of the structured personality combine in the school years to become part of character and are thus increasingly resistant to change from experience or analysis.

Derivatives of such developments appear in adolescent and adult treatments in the quality of the therapeutic alliance and resistance to it. There are particular conflicts that arise mostly in the middle phase of treatments when issues of the capacity to work and to work together in the relationship with the therapist are most salient. Developmental images related to functioning in the school years may surface in the closed-system borderland territory of defensive functioning, where obsessional detailing of stories inhabits the material or excessive punctiliousness in a patient calls to mind a schoolchild preoccupied with lists, collecting and order; conversely, shared gusto at moments of insight, companionable pleasure in hearing about a passion or interest of the patient may evoke images of industrious, dedicated youngsters.

PHASE CHALLENGE: Negotiate rules, rewards, demands, and controls of the external world.

OPEN-SYSTEM RESPONSE: Good feelings from image of self as competent, effective, capable of learning, playing, negotiating, socializing, controlling self, and changing.

<u>Signs</u> include successful mastery of impulses, tolerance of ambivalence, development of complex relationships, capacity for pleasure in work.

CLOSED-SYSTEM RESPONSE: Self-esteem based mainly on belief in control of others; real talents and capacities co-opted to maintain delusional image of omnipotent self (entitlement, exception). <u>Symptoms</u> include persistence of earlier problems, intensification of obsessional rituals alternating with wild, "hyper," anxiety-driven behavior, lack of pleasure in real achievements, learning problems, bullying, victimization, inability to play, social isolation.

7

Adolescence

The youngster who has experienced school years that have consolidated and enhanced real, open-system skills, talents, and pleasure in competent interactions welcomes the growing capacities of mind and body that come with adolescence and open further opportunities for engagement and the increase of self-esteem. This is not to deny that *Mastering ordinary challenges with open-system solutions builds emotional muscle.* adolescence, like all of life, contains disappointment, hurt, failure, and painful realizations of limitations. But the teenager who had a good-enough latency, which includes good-enough parents and environment, can surmount, and may even be strengthened by grappling with, the ordinary obstacles encountered.

On the other hand, an adolescent who has lived in a closed-system, sadomasochistic world, with its costly omnipotent beliefs in quick, easy triumph over others, will be unable to integrate those beliefs with the reality of a changing body and changing external demands. The internal and external realities of adolescence challenge the omnipotent beliefs of the younger child. Adolescent growth, with the capacity to put wishes into real action, demands transformation of earlier closed-system solutions.

All of the developmental tasks of adolescence require a transformation of the relation to reality and fantasy, as part of the integration of the mature body and self. The generally well-functioning adolescent, in the course of integrating his mature body and self, achieves a new integration of the pleasure and reality principles. For the disturbed adolescent, organizing his personality around closed-system solutions, the two remain in opposition, so that what is real is not pleasurable, and pleasure resides in unreal magical fantasies.

We look at a sequence of developmental steps in this arena, moving from acceptance of having a sexual body, to having a gendered body, culminating eventually in consolidating the choice of sexual partner.[36] There is a very broad spectrum of individual variation in adolescence around each of these steps, which makes experiencing, understanding, and assessing development complex. Open-system progression through the steps manifests as summarized in the box at the end of this chapter, whereas closed-system responses tend to attempt to interrupt, slow, or divert the pace of change or stop change itself.

The experience of genital pleasure renders untenable any longer an illusory notion of oedipal equality, and requires acknowledgement of generational differences. Coalescence of a separate identity contradicts the belief in indispensability or identity with parents. Acceptance of the realities of time, choice, and personal limitations necessitates abandoning the fixed magical ideas that one need never grow up, grow old, die, have to choose, or give up anything. The major task of early adolescence is the integration of the maturing body with childhood self-representations and beliefs. Late adolescents have the task of identity formation with its attendant choices, goals, and commitments, including accepting realistic perceptions of themselves and their parents. None of the phase-appropriate tasks can be accomplished while simultaneously maintaining an omnipotent delusion. Once they see their parents clearly, older adolescents are in a position to select those aspects of their parents they want to identify with. Closed-system parent-child relationships conduce to more global, introjective identifications, perpetuating sadomasochistic patterns internally and in other relationships.

Open-system realistic emulation tends to be more conscious and non-defensive; it includes internalization of parenting functions, such as bodily care and management; regulation and control of feelings and impulses; provision of affirmation, validation, love, and praise; setting goals and standards; providing meaning and direction. When parenting functions are taken in and owned, adolescents are in a position to function as adults, whether they actually yet live independently or not.

Thus we can characterize adolescence as a time of challenging conflict between pulls to open- and closed-system functioning. The resolution of the contradiction between the reality demands of adolescence and closed-system omnipotent beliefs determines the outcome of adolescent development and sets the course for adult health or pathology. An adolescent on a realistic path of progressive development opts for the pleasures of reality and sets aside a past or recently-formed closed-system solution. Clinging to the omnipotent solution can lead to avoidance of the actual tasks of adolescence or to an escalating, even self-destructive, series of actions designed to deny reality, attribute responsibility and guilt to others, make others feel helpless and anxious, indeed to enact the omnipotent belief of hostile control over the actions and reactions of others.

We suggest that adolescence is the period when a closed-system, perverse sadomasochistic solution to conflict, with its core omnipotent beliefs, is consolidated as feeling essential to the individual's survival.[37] The choice of a closed-system solution becomes a built-in response of the personality, experienced as increasingly inevitable, taking on addictive force.

> *Over time, closed-system solutions become part of personality structure.*

Each of the strands from earlier levels can be intensified under the impact of the real changes of adolescence. As the adolescent moves or is pushed toward autonomy and independence, and anxiety about issues of attachment, separateness, loneliness, and loss intensifies and threatens traumatic helplessness, so the strand of pain as an omnipotent means of attachment is reinforced. Toddler fears about rage, death, and destruction are revived in the light of the adolescent's real ability to put his killing wishes into action, and so the strand of omnipotent conviction of the capacity to murder can also be intensified. Powerful defenses against intense feelings, indeed, against feeling at all, may be invoked with increasing desperation. Adolescent sexuality can heighten oedipal feelings of rejection, humiliation, envy and jealousy, and thus the strand of delusional belief in the power and irresistibility of sexual urges is further strengthened. The latency need to externalize the conscience and avoid responsibility and guilt is intensified by adolescent incestuous and perverse wishes; the strand of quick, externally imposed, immediate gratifications is also thereby thickened.

We can characterize adolescence as a time of leave-taking, whether literally from the primary family and home, or internally and symbolically in the farewell to childhood. We have noted that patterns of their adolescent leave-taking are often repeated in how individuals leave treatment. To us this represents another example of the importance of thinking developmentally and knowing what the open- and closed-system options and patterns are at different times in the life cycle. Echoes and derivatives from each phase affect and are affected by each other phase and will appear in later life and in treatment.

In adolescence the strands from all the prior developmental phases can become braided into what seems like an unbreakable rope of closed-system functioning clung to as a defense against the danger of experienced threats of annihilation, abandonment, humiliation, castration, rage, jealousy, and guilt. It is during adolescence that omnipotent beliefs are either superseded by open-system, reality-based modes of self-regulation or become fixed as a delusional core of a diverse range of adolescent and adult pathology, from the apparently normally-functioning obsessional neurotic to the perverse, addicted, impulse-driven, narcissistically-damaged borderline personality disorder.

PHASE CHALLENGE: Real changes in body, mind, and social expectations

OPEN-SYSTEM RESPONSE: Ownership of mature, sexual body; consolidation of gender identity; realistic self- and object-representations.

Signs include pleasure in appearance and functioning of body; increase in capacity to parent self, constant relationships with peers.

CLOSED-SYSTEM RESPONSE: Maintenance of omnipotent beliefs by means of increasingly desperate self-destructive actions. Symptoms include: pathological use of the body (eating disorders, self-mutilation, suicide, substance abuse, pregnancy, repeated abortion, rapid repeat pregnancy, promiscuity); addiction, bullying, delinquency, depression, personality fragmentation, low achievement, grandiosity, social isolation, persistent immaturity.

8

Young Adulthood

In line with psychoanalytic thinkers from Erikson[38] on, we think development continues throughout adulthood and into *Development spans the whole life cycle.* old age to the end of life.[39] It follows then that we suggest that each stage of adult life brings particular phase challenges, and that individuals may respond to those with either open- or closed-system methods of regulating themselves and resolving conflicts.

Consolidation of character formation and preponderance of open- or closed-system responses in late adolescence set the scene for adult functioning and determine much of the course of young adulthood and its tasks of engaging in life and work through choices of career and partner. For many years social scientists have suggested considering young adulthood as an extended period of late adolescence. Support for that position has come from neuro-developmental studies that show that rapid brain development proceeds until at least age 26.[40] Our experience, however, confirms Laufer's insight that it seems important to maintain some distinction between adolescence and young adulthood, in order not to lose sight of critical distinctions that may be diagnostically important in looking at adolescents.[41] We think it is also possible to discern different core challenges in the two stages. Thus we think of late adolescence as encompassing the undergraduate/apprentice years (approximately 17 – 21 years of age) and young adulthood comprising the twenties.

Each young adult is faced with the challenge of sustaining a secure sense of a separate self, as well as maintaining creativity, intimacy, and growth in the face of potential helplessness and hurt from rejection, disappointment, frustration, or accidents of fate. Just as in earlier phases, individuals may respond in an open- or closed-system way.

In late adolescence many can make a closed-system choice to avoid the reality of experiencing separateness by equating physical proximity and shared values with the illusion of being one with a larger group (family, gang, fraternity, couple, college, fan and so forth). But this is hard to maintain after graduation/apprenticeship; each person is challenged by the essential separateness of each individual. *Every person is challenged by the essential separateness of individuals.* Loneliness is a feeling that inevitably arises with experience of separateness. People can respond to loneliness in an open- or closed-system way.

Closed-system responses are designed to deny and block out the experience of loneliness, since it is likely to feel like an unbearable pain. Young adults may resort to a closed-system response, as in substance abuse, depression, suicide or mind-numbing behaviors, such as obsessional mechanisms and compulsions, or dissociation. Frantic, driven behavior and shallow or promiscuous relationships may be used to defend against loneliness omnipotently equated with rejection, humiliation, or abandonment.[42]

Open-system responses conduce to and consist of accepting the experience of loneliness as intrinsic to a transitional phase in life, thereby underscoring a realistic relationship to time. Young adults can use "self-talk," saying, for instance, 'this pain is temporary,' 'things change,' 'the future is not the same as the past or present,' and so forth. Loneliness can be a spur to creative pursuit of interests, meaningful friendships and, eventually, significant and intimate partnerships.

As we consider developmental phases, including the subphases of adulthood, we think it is important to keep in mind our basic assumption of the developmental principle of epigenesis, which posits that any developmental outcome results from an interaction between psychobiological givens and the impact of external factors that include cultural, economic, political, historical and biophysiological changes, such as is known to occur in the middle twenties. In Italy, for example, young adults usually live at home with their families into their thirties (la familia lunga). Issues of autonomy, self-care, and significant relationships with others may be thereby obscured. Nevertheless the internal developmental tasks still have to be engaged with and mastered.[43]

For women the challenge of work and career choice varies with culture and access to education. In large parts of the world women's jobs are restricted to household, childbearing and child rearing responsibilities. In the US and many first world countries young women are acculturated to expect to have both a career and a family, although attitudes of many North American men and businesses, and labor regulations remain 60 years behind the times in facilitating this dimension. Nevertheless, both young adult men and women face the challenge of career choice at this phase. While many external factors affect life path for young adults, we think that the two-systems model offers a useful perspective in contributing to understanding the complexities of development in young adulthood.

We noted in the last chapter that late adolescents using open-system modes of self-regulation have set aside magical, omnipotent self-representations and can accept realistic goals, choices and commitments. Most high school athletes accept that they will never be professionals and turn their attention elsewhere. With open-system realism, invested with pleasure in experiences of mastery of real challenges, people can assess their passions, interests and skills to see what jobs will enhance their capacities and give pleasure. If no such job exists, they may do as Freud did, or Mark Zuckerberg did, or what members of the Alliance for Psychoanalytic Schools did – they can create a new category of work.[44]

If closed-system solutions continue to play a significant role, the young adult will not find any work satisfying, will find it hard or impossible to develop skills to use with pleasure, will remain unhappy, resentful, complaining and most likely underfunctioning. In an extension of adolescent patterns, the young adult operating with closed-system responses may search for satisfaction from quick and easy sources, like excessive drinking, "partying," drugs and drug dealing, or other marginal or illegal activities. In extreme forms, this can devolve to being a terrorist or killer.

PHASE CHALLENGE: Engaging with the reality of internal needs and external demands to find partner and career.
OPEN-SYSTEM RESPONSE: Using emotional muscles to tolerate risks and stresses of life choices; working on enhancing skills for life and work.
CLOSED-SYSTEM RESPONSE: resisting change, denying time, avoiding life tasks.

9

Adulthood

The years between approximately 30 and 50 are complex and multifaceted. The central challenge is to achieve the phase of parenthood, and traverse its subphases of progressive development. We characterize parenthood in terms of creativity, generativity, and mentorship, in the sustained motivation and capacity to invest deeply in and nurture someone or something beyond the self, whether or not the individual actually has children. The characteristics of this phase may be seen vividly in relation to actual children, but responses to these challenges apply equally to other endeavors, such as starting a business, writing a book, designing a new course, training apprentices, managing others, directing a play and so forth.

We can look at the first task in parenthood as a paradigm of possible responses to the general challenges of the phase of adulthood (see also our earlier chapter on Pregnancy). An initial potential source of feeling helpless is the reality of the separateness of each individual. A newborn baby is actually a stranger whom one has to get to know. Mother and baby can be partners in their mutual learning about each other in an open- or closed-system way. Parenting partners can draw upon their own open-system emotional muscles for resources of patience and perseverance; or they can draw the tasks into a sadomasochistic interaction with each other and invoke closed-system defenses, for instance using the infant as a target for externalizations.

Essential open-system emotional muscles for adults include tolerating failure and the reality of limitations. If this is built on lifelong practice, the challenge is not so great and the threat of danger will not be felt as overwhelming. Taking in the knowledge, for instance, that parents and infants in even optimal situations are "attuned" only 30% of the time supports realistic standards for the self, combating closed-system perfectionism and self-torture around not being ideal parents.

> *Tolerating failure and accepting the reality of limitations are essential open-system emotional muscles for adults.*

Learning to repair the mismatch provides experiences of competence and mastery to baby and parents, fueling a self-representation grounded in real open-system capacities. The parallels to setting personal standards and meeting external goals in other contexts are clear.

Just as the reality of adolescent development can stimulate setting aside omnipotent solutions, so the reality of parenthood in adult life can lead to restructuring values and consolidation of an open-system conscience. Progressive development as an adult shows in increased flexibility and complexity of judgments, tolerance of self and others, and the ability to set a good example. Predominantly open-system functioning includes a realistic sense of agency and a willingness to own both achievements and failures.

A closed-system response, as we have seen at earlier phases of development, often includes all-or-nothing thinking, which makes it hard to tolerate ambiguity, ambivalence or mixed feelings. The experience of being needed is highly gratifying, in the family or the workplace. An open-system response to the challenges of this phase demonstrates altruism and responsibility, and evolution of values based on real experience, while maintaining core principles in the ego ideal, ideal self, and conscience. Pleasure comes from a sense of making a contribution, having real impact.

With open-system emotional muscles, an adult can simultaneously enjoy being needed and acknowledge that the goal of parenting or mentoring or nurturing is to foster autonomy. The sequence of steps in encouraging autonomy – doing for, doing with, standing by to admire, then independent functioning – includes the adult being able to bear the sadness at leaving the earlier stages behind, along with appreciating and enjoying the freedom it brings.[45] This sequence repeats with each developmental step mastered by a child, or each stage of progression of a project. Ultimately adults responding in an open-system way come to embrace the reality that development involves transformation in all parties, and that transformation of relationships continues throughout life.

Closed-system functioning in adulthood comprises many different symptom pictures in multiple diagnostic categories, with emphasis on sadomasochistic, omnipotent beliefs and their pervasive impact. Rigidity, harshness, black-and-white thinking, zero-sum ideas all indicate the operation of closed-system ego and superego self-regulation. Perfectionism and delinquency can alternate or coexist, along with habitual tendencies to blame others and attribute responsibility to the outside.

We have named parenthood as the main phase challenge of adulthood, whether a person has actual children or not. Another way to characterize the difference between open- and closed-system responses to this multifarious challenge is by contrasting authoritative parenting with authoritarian parenting. Our clinical experience has demonstrated that closed-system sadomasochism can be sequestered and lived out in parenting in otherwise relatively well-functioning adults. The power differential of the parent-child relationship or some workplace conditions may offer an easy context for playing out closed-system dynamics, interactions and patterns.[46]

Closed-system sado-masochism can be sequestered and concealed in parenting.

PHASE CHALLENGE: creativity and generativity beyond oneself (parenthood).

OPEN-SYSTEM RESPONSE: engaging with the reality of growth, transformation, limitations; tolerating uncertainty; patience, tolerance, perseverance, altruism, flexibility; ownership of actions and self.

CLOSED-SYSTEM RESPONSE: rigidity, harshness, perfectionism; black-and-white thinking; authoritarianism; externalization of blame and responsibility.

10

Middle Age

W e see change and transience as the major developmental challenges in middle age.[47] All people have to deal with alterations in their bodies, minds and relationships, creating pressure for transformations in the self-representation. Those with families also face aging in older parents and siblings, growth and transformation in their children, and changes in their roles in relation to all these different people. The central fact is growing awareness of the limitations of time and the reality of mortality. Unpredictability, unfamiliarity and uncertainty is part of all this, carrying the danger of helplessness. Just as at any earlier challenging moment in development, individuals can respond in open- and closed-system ways in the effort to reestablish a sense of safety, connection and pleasure.

An open-system response to the challenge of internal and external changes includes taking pleasure in realistic assessment of oneself and others. Liking and accepting one's virtues and flaws means coming to terms with reality. Thinking about what can be changed, worked on, or attempted can co-exist with acceptance of the consequences of life choices and those things that one cannot control. Accessing a capacity to mourn engages with the changes taking place at all levels, from alterations in one's sexual nature, differences in leadership roles at work, primacy as a parent transmuting to the grandparent role; mourning facilitates access to pleasure in the evolving new roles.

Open-system responses can be discerned in the pleasure taken in new creative endeavors, engaging in community service (this extends the care for others begun in earlier adulthood), and enjoyment of the growth of adolescent and young adult children. Mentorship, while leading to self-replacement, can also be deeply satisfying, as using knowledge and sharing skills are what Erikson meant by "generativity."[48] Accepting the limitations of time can lead to reordering of priorities and the savoring of experience.

A closed-system response, in contrast, shows in a decrease of tolerance and increased rigidity regarding oneself and others,. A range of pathological defenses may become more evident during this phase, with denial, externalization and projection prominent. Denial of the passage of time and the vulnerability of the body may show in the development of addictions to alcohol, drugs, or medications, fad dieting, fanatical exercise, pursuit of cosmetic surgery, as well as in acting out of fantasies through affairs, precipitate divorce – all the signs of what is popularly termed the "midlife crisis."[49]

Parents of adolescents and young adults often seem to struggle with changes in their children, reacting to burgeoning sexuality, maturity and life potential with closed-system defenses and acting out to deny the waning of their own powers. Unable to accept the changes in their own body, blame is often externalized onto changes in the outside world, located in a spouse, social and cultural shifts, with respite or rescue sought in increasingly extreme solutions. The sadomasochistic aspect of closed-system solutions becomes visible, for instance, in enthrallment with a new young partner, or submission to a powerful religious or political figure.

PHASE CHALLENGE: Change and transience; mortality.
OPEN-SYSTEM RESPONSE: Pleasure from realistic assessment of self and others; acceptance of mortality with enjoyment of time left.
CLOSED-SYSTEM RESPONSE: decreased tolerance, increased rigidity; denial of change and death; rage and blame at externalized foci. Search for rescue and respite in sadomasochistic enthrallment to outside figures.

11

Old Age

In old age, waning powers face each of us with the challenge of coming to terms with mortality. There is no more 'plenty of time', unlimited opportunity, multiple possibilities, and so forth. Erikson posed the challenge in terms of a choice between maintaining ego integrity and succumbing to despair. In two-systems terms, we describe the alternatives of realistic, open-system responses and closed-system defenses against the helplessness of despair.

Open-system responses include taking opportunities to share experience, knowledge, skills, and wealth with others in all generations. Recognizing that time is not unlimited promotes efforts to make reparation for faults or past bad actions. Taking pleasure in having lived a life as best one could directly combats despair and feelings of futility. Similarly, assessing realistically what is still possible in one's own work, in care of others, in contribution to society, in aesthetic experiences, in present consciousness of satisfactions large and small – all offer resources of good feelings.

The role reversal that occurs between aged parents and their children poses another challenge, involving both acceptance of a new differential of powers and capacities and the opportunity for further transformation of the relationship. The possibility of continuing to serve as a role model in engaging with the challenges of this new phase of development can be deeply satisfying.

Closed-system responses show in bitterness and regret. Dealing with the helplessness of inevitable outcomes by denial of the reality of time and mortality conduces to internal permission for destructive rage at younger people, including one's own children or grandchildren. A psychologically similar response, although it appears to be the opposite, can be abdication, using all-or-nothing thinking to feel completely impotent, incapable and irresponsible. Milder forms of closed-system defensive omnipotent entitlement appear in license for rudeness, prejudice against societal change, unfamiliar people, technology, and/or rejection of appropriate help and concern from others.

PHASE CHALLENGE: Physical decline; mortality.

OPEN-SYSTEM RESPONSE: Pleasure in remaining capacities, in a life well-lived, ongoing shared pleasures; transformation of relationships.

CLOSED-SYSTEM RESPONSE: bitterness, despair, denial; externalizations of blame and criticism; entitlement.

II

Treatment

12

Phases and Tasks of Treatment

In Part I we used the two-systems model to look at responses to the challenges of development at different stages. In Part II we will look at the two-systems model as it applies to clinical technique through the phases of treatment.

We hope to demonstrate how keeping a two-system model in mind can organize a therapist's technical approaches, enhancing the technical repertoire and expanding the range of clinical interventions.

There is understandable reluctance in analysts to categorizing of patients or to manualizing treatment into some generic format. Each patient forms a unique relationship with each analyst, who in turn changes with and is changed by each patient. The course of each analysis is also unique, unpredictable, and perhaps more amenable to chaos theory than two-dimensional linear regression coefficients. Metapsychological (or multidimensional) descriptions of mental phenomena are appropriately complex, however clearly they can be made. At the same time, from Freud's early distinctions between passive and active seductions, primary and secondary process thinking, the delineation of the sequence of libidinal phases, and his recommendations to analysts for the beginning of analysis, the heuristic value of categorization has been accepted.[50] Freud discussed the beginning phase of analysis and referred to the middle and end phases, but it was Glover who much later explicitly suggested segmenting analysis into beginning, middle and termination phases.[51] As we have tried to understand that idea, it seems that we need also to think about *how* treatment moves or proceeds through such phases.

Inherent in Erikson's theory of the life cycle, Freud's concepts of drive theory and psychosexual stages, and Anna Freud's developmental lines is the idea of direction.[52] All child analysts explicitly or implicitly use developmental goals as standards in their diagnoses, assessments, treatment plans, and termination decisions. Anna Freud's overarching treatment goal of restoration to the path of progressive development is a clear statement of direction and movement. This has led us to apply a developmental point of view to the trajectory of therapy. We see treatment as a developmental experience for patient, therapist and significant others. Thinking in this way about development and direction leads to conceptualizing treatment goals. For us the central goal is the freedom to choose how to deal with life's challenges from inside or outside. The active pursuit of that goal with our patients allows therapists to expand technique, as we describe in the chapters that follow on each phase of treatment. It allows us to formulate a definition of psychoanalysis and psychotherapy as multidimensional, using multimodal techniques.

> *Treatment is a developmental experience for all parties.*

Erikson extended Freud's idea of phases of psychosexual development to the "eight stages of man," each with its own particular organ modes, social modalities and nuclear conflicts.[53] At each developmental stage he described the ego as faced with the task of finding a solution to that conflict. When we apply those ideas to treatment, we can think of psychoanalysis in terms of phases, therapeutic tasks, and assessment of accomplishment of those tasks, or the outcome of therapeutic interventions at any given point in the treatment. We speak of each treatment phase having its own nuclear conflict or task to master that is experienced by everyone.

The patient's ego has the task of solving that conflict, accomplishing that task. How he solves it reveals particulars of the individual patient's history and current functioning and

Each phase of treatment has its own major task.

how the analyst responds varies with the skill, training, and orientation of the individual analyst. But everyone is faced with the same basic challenges, for instance, at evaluation, where the task is to resolve the conflict between being and not being a patient; at the beginning of treatment, the dilemma for everyone is about how to feel safe enough to be with the therapist, and so on through the phases of treatment.

Some psychoanalytic writers have suggested that there is an actual recapitulation of earlier development in the course of therapy.[54] In accordance with our epigenetic approach that posits constant interaction among internal and external factors and temporal impact both forward and backwards, however, we think that equation was oversimplified. In all our writings we have described the layering of experience from each stage of life, the intertwining of strands of derivatives from earlier phases operative in the present.[55]

At the end of each chapter in Part I of the book (Development), we summarized in a box the particular challenge of each developmental phase and closed- and open-system responses. In the next chapter, we will be describing the sequence of therapeutic alliance tasks highlighted at each phase of treatment. There are parallels between them, which suggests that we should consider more closely the nature of the developmental experience of treatment. At this point we are thinking in a preliminary way that each treatment phase predominantly evokes resonances, echoes, or derivatives of earlier modes of functioning from a particular developmental phase. We will explore the nature of those parallels in more detail in the chapters on each treatment phase in this section of the book. Here, however, we suggest some further general points.

Closed-system development seems generally to follow a somewhat linear path. The active search for pain of the adult sadomasochistic patient most likely started in infancy when pain became associated

Closed-system functioning is more linear and predictive than open-system.

with attachment. We have found that toddler, preschool, schoolage, and adolescent derivatives all reappear at later phases – "old wine in new bottles." Each phase challenge noted in the boxes can be discerned in adult form later on. Established closed-system functioning is relatively unaffected by external reality, with old solutions clung to despite new circumstances and opportunities. This may mean that the developmental resonances that seem specific to any one treatment phase are likely to relate more to closed- than open-system aspects. We will use examples from our published and unpublished work of the past fifty years as illustrations later in the book.

Open-system functioning, on the other hand, seems less linear, not clearly predictive of later behavior or functioning. Open-system modes of self-regulation are in constant epigenetic interaction with changing internal capacities, external opportunities and outside influences. Thus we may expect to see less correspondence between specific developmental phases and particular treatment phases in relation to open-system factors.

At the beginning of treatment each patient has an individual way of functioning, some struggling to begin, others overflowing with material. But, with all patients, we therapists really do not yet have enough sure knowledge to make substantive interpretations. That uncertainty can feel like a kind of helplessness; therapists, just like everyone else, can respond in open- or closed-system ways. We have talked about a tolerance for uncertainty as one of the most important "emotional muscles" for therapists.[56] Equipped with sturdy emotional muscles, replenished from a robust personal emotional life, we can also call upon a range of models of mental functioning to orient ourselves in the initially chartless expanse of meeting a new person and entering a relationship of unknown potential.

A schema of phases of treatment, with characteristic tasks, just like a model of two systems of self-regulation, can help to protect therapists from taking refuge in closed-system thinking and reacting. Such maps can ground us in the reality of the experienced relationship with the patient, keeping us from the covert hostility of excessive therapeutic ambition or closed-system thoughtless adherence to artificial rules. Closed-system reactions in therapists can take the sadomasochistic form of authoritarian imposition of fixed ideas or theories on the patient, an assault on the patient's closely-held defenses by premature or too deep interpretations, or longer-term enmeshment in an exploitative power relationship.

The tasks of the therapeutic alliance, each highlighted particularly in different phases of treatment, offer a useful framework in themselves for understanding conflicts, defenses, resistances and possibilities. Even more importantly, we have come to see that mastery of therapeutic alliance tasks both fosters and springs from open-system functioning. In the next section, we will discuss therapeutic alliance tasks at each phase in more detail.

Mastery of therapeutic alliance tasks comes from and leads to open-system functioning.

13

The Therapeutic Alliance and Its Tasks Through the Phases of Treatment

The therapeutic alliance is a psychoanalytic concept that goes back to the very beginnings of psychoanalysis.[57] It rose to prominence in psychoanalytic thinking with the development of ego psychology in Vienna in the 1930's and was crystallized as an essential component of treatment by Greenson and others in the 1970's.[58] Outside psychoanalysis, the alliance concept continues to hold a central place with other mental health professionals, while it has fallen somewhat into abeyance, even disfavor, in 21st-century mainstream psychoanalytic thinking.

From Freud's formulations through to the work of Greenson and those who espoused his description, the alliance between patient and analyst has been seen in terms of an interpersonal relationship. It has always assumed a two-person psychology.[59] We think that the dismissal of the alliance concept as ambiguous, specious, or dangerous was a loss to our field. It deprived classical, mainstream psychoanalytic theory of a conceptual vehicle for integrating the relational and cognitive-affective components of analysis. This allowed for the emergence of divergent schools created in opposition or reaction to a technique seen as sterile, inhumane, and incompatible with an object-relational, interpersonal, or intersubjective two-person psychology.

We, on the other hand, have always found that we could not do without some kind of alliance concept, particularly when we attempted to make sense of complex clinical phenomena in apparently very different areas of theoretical exploration. Our studies of termination describe the therapeutic alliance as a crucial indicator during the pretermination phase of readiness to start a termination phase, and as a central factor in an adaptive response to termination itself.[60] The capacity for self-analysis, currently formulated as a major goal of analysis itself, can be understood as a result of the internalization of the therapeutic alliance. Our work on sadomasochism, omnipotence, and externalization led to a view of the alliance tasks at each phase of treatment as a way of highlighting the resistances of sadomasochism.[61] Our continued need for and sense of the utility of an alliance concept has led us to a revised theory of the therapeutic alliance, in which we attempt to integrate the contributions of the many theorists who have grappled with the issues involved.[62]

Our revised theory of the therapeutic alliance is operationalized in terms of specific tasks for each person in the therapeutic relationship – therapist, patient, and parents or significant others.[63] All the therapeutic alliance tasks persist throughout treatment, but specific tasks come to the forefront in each phase. This formulation of the therapeutic alliance has proved useful as a lens for highlighting certain features of the therapeutic relationship and some pervasive aspects of pathology, particularly closed-system, sadomasochistic. omnipotent resistances and relationships in treatment.

Here, briefly summarized below, are the main general points of our conceptualization of the therapeutic alliance. In later chapters on each phase of treatment, we will discuss in detail the therapeutic alliance tasks of that phase and their interaction with other ways of perceiving and thinking about the material.

- *The therapeutic alliance as a lens*
  The therapeutic alliance is not different or separate from other traditional technical perspectives on the therapeutic process; it is as useful a way of looking at clinical data as are, for instance, transference, resistance, defense analysis, and so forth. The concept of the therapeutic alliance is like a lens that highlights certain features of the material. It is the same material whichever lens is used. Looking through the lens of the alliance particularly focuses our attention on open-system capacities and functioning, in contrast to closed-system functioning that generally reveals itself in transference-countertransference interactions.

- *Ego capacities and motives*
  It is useful to distinguish between those capacities necessary for an alliance and the motivation to use those capacities for mutually agreed therapeutic goals. Most patients, including children and adolescents, have the capacities of thought and feeling necessary for a therapeutic alliance. Individual differences among patients are found in relation to motivations. Failure to make this distinction creates false divisions among patients, between patients and therapists, and provides therapists with an excuse for treatment failure. Our experience with severely disturbed patients of all ages has been that they are able to build and maintain an alliance when that is made an integral part of the therapeutic endeavor. The closed-system tendency to co-opt good ego capacities in the service of maintaining omnipotent beliefs, sadomasochistic relationships, and pathological defenses is evident in interferences with the alliance.

- *Motives for the therapeutic alliance*
  The therapeutic alliance is motivated by rational and irrational forces, including the transference to treatment of adaptive and maladaptive earlier psychic organizations. Motives will be

77

conscious and unconscious, springing from both id desires and legitimate ego needs.[64] Id desires tend to emerge on their own; the ego needs must be acknowledged and tapped into actively by the therapist to support the therapy. In work with all age groups, it is unnecessary initially to distinguish between rational and irrational, mature or infantile motives for the alliance. These are value judgments that lead to a conceptual muddle and technical paralysis. Experience with children teaches us to take what we can get and use it to the fullest while it is there. Technique is guided, in part, by a search for motives to start and maintain an alliance, an alertness to closed-system resistances that interfere with the alliance and a constant awareness of the instability of the alliance.

- *Fluctuations in the alliance*
  The therapeutic alliance has been generally described by adult analysts as a stable force in the therapeutic situation, to be depended on throughout the treatment. In our experience, the therapeutic alliance is not stable, but varies at different stages of treatment and, more microscopically, with each successive emergence of a conflict and its relational, affective and drive components. To take this further, the fluctuations of the alliance enable the therapist to see, share, and interpret conflict, defense, anxiety and transference in a way the patient, even a young child, can understand. Fluctuations in the alliance may be used as a barometer of conflict, resistance and change, as we will examine in more detail in the chapters to come.

- *Therapeutic alliance as a relationship*
  The therapeutic alliance is a relational concept; as such, it requires input from all parties to it. Usually this includes patient, therapist, and parents or significant others, each of whom has a complementary phase-appropriate task. Here, too, rational and irrational, conscious and unconscious,

transference and non-transference elements of relationships are all included.

- *Tasks of the therapeutic alliance*
  The treatment phases and their alliance tasks are summarized in the table on the following page. The table is organized for ease of reading as a grid, but it should be kept in mind that the therapeutic alliance tasks of each phase persist through all subsequent phases. Resistance may be seen in relation to any of the alliance tasks, but the primary task highlighted in each phase relates to the progression of the therapeutic work through the course of treatment and provides a measure of that progress. Accomplishment of therapeutic alliance tasks correlates with activation of and exercise of open-system capacities.

  All the alliance tasks persist through all treatment phases

THERAPEUTIC ALLIANCE TASKS

	EVALUATION	BEGINNING	MIDDLE	PRETERMINATION	TERMINATION	POST-TERM
Patient	Bring material Engage in transformation tasks	Being with therapist	Working together with therapist	Putting insights into action Independent therapeutic work Maintain progressive momentum	Setting aside omnipotent beliefs Internalization of alliance Mourning	Use alliance skills for living and creativity
Therapist	Initiate transformations of: • self-help to joint work • chaos to order and meaning • fantasies to realistic goals • external complaints to internal conflicts • despair to hope • helplessness to competence • guilt to usable concern	Feeling with patient	Maximum use of ego functions	Allow for patient's independent therapeutic work	Allow patient's mourning Deal with own loss Analyze to end	Stay available as analyst Allow continued growth Grow with patient
Parents or Signif. other	Engage in and allow transformations	Allow the being with	Allow for individuation or psychological separation	Enjoy and validate progression	Mourning loss of therapy Internalization of alliance Consolidation in phase of parenthood	

14

Two Systems and the Therapeutic Alliance

O pen-system functioning is a potential response to life's challenges at any time. It takes work, activity, engagement with the
world and other people. Closed-system functioning is a potential
choice of response to perceived danger, threat, challenge at any point
in development. In the face of overwhelming experience, anyone
may resort to a closed-system response, whatever their earlier history
and habitual mode of self-regulation may be. Our clinical experience
demonstrates, however, that a closed-system response often has deep
and pervasive roots that grow from repeated and compounded
experience at multiple levels of development.

Given that background of layered, structured, and habitual, often addicted, response to stress in most patients who present with
sadomasochistic, self-defeating or self-destructive personalities, it
follows that we do not see closed-system sadomasochistic functioning in treatment as largely a product of something co-created
with the analyst.

- Closed-system functioning is not caused by the therapist.
  It is how the patient has functioned throughout development, probably since infancy, now generalized to all

relationships. It is a "generalized transference," in which the patient tries to engage the therapist in a familiar sadomasochistic relationship.

- The therapist has the difficult task of perceiving and understanding the patient's closed-system functioning, but not being pulled into either side of the dominance / submission dynamic.
- The therapist is a representative of reality as actualized in the tasks of the therapeutic alliance. As such, the therapist helps the patient begin to experience an alternative mode of self-regulation and relationship in the open system.
- The tasks of the therapeutic alliance at each phase of treatment operationalize open-system functioning – they are the objective correlative of the open system.
- The therapist actively engages the patient in each phase's tasks, nurturing the alliance by verbalizing resistances, tracing sources of resistance, finding the legitimate need met by the closed-system defense, and helping the patient find less costly and more effective ways to meet real needs.
- This sequence repeats through each treatment phase as the patient internalizes open-system alternatives to costly, closed-system defenses.
- After multiple iterations of testing, dealing with feelings about setting aside omnipotent solutions, and internalizing effective and competent modes of open-system self-regulation, patients are in a position of freedom to choose between the two modes of self-regulation.
- Having worked together to restore the freedom to choose, patient and therapist can prepare for a good goodbye.

15

Two Systems and
Two Techniques

The two-system formulation leads to delineating two kinds of technique.[65] Expanding our repertoire of interventions is an important benefit of this rethinking of a psychoanalytic developmental model. Convergence and integration of a variety of approaches take place in practical terms through the application of the framework of our revised theory of the therapeutic alliance, with its phase-specific tasks for each party to a treatment.

Technical interventions have differing impacts on phenomena relating to the two systems. Closed-system phenomena require the drive/defense, classical approach of *Closed-system functioning requires classical technique.* transference and resistance analysis, with the aim of putting the patient in the active center of his pathology. But defense and transference interpretations of open-system functioning can pathologize and drive away competence.

Mirroring, empathy, reconstruction, validation, support, and developmental education, to list but a few, link open-system phenomena with the analyst's functions beyond serving only as a transference object. These techniques applied to closed-system functioning, however, may be at best a palliative waste of time; at worst, they may serve to reinforce a passive, helpless, victimized stance on the part of the patient. Thus, we have to think in terms of expanded

Open-system functioning demands expanded and alternative techniques.

and alternative technical options to encompass the open-system dimensions of our patients' personalities and the opportunities of the treatment situation.

What are the technical interventions that illuminate the operation of each system, that address resistances and nurture open-system alternatives in the day-to-day work of treatment? In the next section of the book, each chapter about a particular phase of treatment will address three dimensions of technique in relation to both open- and closed-system functioning.

The first concerns *what we attend to*. We want to consider how the two-systems model affects our choices, both conscious and preconscious, of what to listen for. The second is the *actual interventions* we make or don't make. Here belong issues of timing, tact, order – how we decide what to do at a particular moment. Third is what this model allows us *to include* as technique that is specifically and legitimately psychoanalytic.

WHAT DO WE ATTEND TO?

We suggest that analysts generally attend to as much as they can, perceiving at many levels material of all kinds generated in interaction with patients. But without a framework much of what is perceived slips into the preconscious and is used or not depending on the personal predilections of the individual analyst. The human tendency to simplify is sometimes intensified by analysts creating a rigid analytic superego that sees different conceptualizations as mutually exclusive, even adversarial, rather than enriching and encompassable within the complex, multidimensional tradition of psychoanalytic theory that looks at human phenomena from many points of view. We can too easily lose the comprehensive metapsychological theory that provides a vocabulary or conceptual framework for the full range of what patients bring and the spectrum of how we intervene.[66]

WHAT DO WE ACTUALLY DO?

Each treatment phase chapter will describe and illustrate actual interventions and our reasons for them. The effort is to generate techniques *We work with both systems throughout.* that engage simultaneously with both closed-system and open-system functioning in relation to the tasks of the phase. Actual interventions are implied in what we attend to, but we can be more explicit about the relation between the two-system model and what we do and say. We don't believe that what we do is foreign or very different from what all experienced analysts do. But a two-system model anchors these interventions in a theoretical framework, one that takes us back to a basic psychoanalytic metapsychological model. It provides an inclusive basis for teaching and describing the range of therapeutic interventions, bringing technical assumptions into the foreground for examination.

Because each analyst's implicit model of development informs what gets attended to we have tried to articulate our dual-track conceptualization of the developmental potential for open- and closed-system self-regulation at every level. Similarly, each person's model of the treatment process affects technical choices. For many these models are seldom articulated but nevertheless have an impact on their view of the patient and the subsequent unfolding of material. The impact of the observer on the observed has now become an analytic and scientific given, but there is too little attention paid to the impact of the analyst's internal working and theoretical models on the patient.

A two-system model offers a theoretical basis for techniques.

Kleinian patients have Kleinian dreams; oedipalists have patients who live in triangular worlds of rivalry, jealousy, triumph and defeat; self psychologists have patients who exhibit basic self deficits and so forth. We contend that it is important to be aware internally about one's model, keeping the model in the open system where it is in constant interaction with the external world, ever open to modification and change.

WHAT TECHNIQUE IS PSYCHOANALYTIC?

Many analytic controversies, splits and dissensions revolve around issues of training and technique. What is psychoanalysis and who can be called a psychoanalyst are issues that continue to exercise psychoanalysts. In our thinking we have always used a metapsychological framework and we have tried in various writings to address how lost or prematurely discarded analytic ideas can be reclaimed and ideas from other approaches can be integrated for fruitful use in reinvigorating our field. Collecting and collating here the techniques we have described in the context of thinking over the past twenty years within a two-systems framework is a further extension of that effort.

16

Evaluation

In this and subsequent chapters, as we proceed through the phases of treatment, we will describe the overall therapeutic alliance task and the specific tasks for patients, therapists, and significant others. We feel that what happens in the evaluation phase is crucial to how the treatment will unfold. Therefore, we describe technique and timing in greater detail in this chapter. We demonstrate how and why we think evaluations should be long enough to create a solid enough base for mutual commitment to a treatment. This includes at least the beginnings of open-system positive feelings of reality-based respect and regard. These are the building blocks of the objective love that will fuel open-system expansion and growth.

LANDFALL/INITIAL CONTACT

We tried to find a word or phrase that would capture first contacts with a potential patient. There are important things that can and should happen from the very start. Therapy is often described as a journey of exploration, which made us think of a time before sophisticated navigational instruments, like the 17th century, when brave or foolhardy adventurers sailed across the unknown oceans hoping for a "good" landfall but prepared for the opposite.

Landfall, the first sighting of land, also connects with our view that the closed system operates in a "borderland," a place rather than a diagnosis.[67] Those who come to see us are feeling overwhelmed, helpless, or anxious, and thereby prone to use closed-system modes of self-regulation and self-protection. Whether we want to or not, we will be inevitably pulled into the borderland and become part of the patient's closed-system efforts for safety, control and gratification.

It is well known and demonstrated in large scale studies that most cases never follow through beyond the initial contact or end soon after, usually refusing the recommendation. This is true in all areas of care. Medical doctors refer to the low rate of adherence to medical regimens and therapists refer to a lack of a therapeutic alliance.[68] This is a public health problem and is also a *Most patients drop out early from all kinds of treatments.* major cause of therapist burnout. Many protect themselves by using treatment modalities that distance them from the patient, like medication, manualized CBT, DBT, MBT and so forth. Those interventions may have their place at times in a multimodal treatment but first we have to make landfall.

We will have to enter the "borderland" but we can only do so safely if we have some idea of the whole territory. The two-system model gives the therapist a rough map of the closed system, the borderland. The open-system tasks of the therapeutic alliance equip us to explore further beyond and describe a path for the journey. In order to travel safely in such difficult, complex, and sometimes dangerous territory, the analyst needs to be supported by concepts that allow him to track the voyage of the treatment.

FIRST PHONE CALL

First, we ensure that there is time to have an initial phone conversation. We ask if this is a good time to talk, "so that we can see the best way to proceed." If it's not convenient, we plan another time.

Respecting the patient's real time constraints to find a mutually available time immediately conveys that we want to work together, one of the first steps in establishing a working alliance.

All patients carry fantasies and expectations about therapists and therapy; these can create a de facto conscious or unconscious treatment plan in the patient's mind. We have

All patients bring their own treatment plan.

found that if this is not addressed from the beginning, the patient's plan will sooner or later take precedence over the therapist's and obviate collaborative efforts to arrive at shared treatment goals and structures.

This is a typical initial call when the patient's plan is explicit: "I was given your name by Dr. X and I am calling to ask if you have time for treatment. Dr. X suggested that I need 2 times per week, continuing my medication, and, oh, by the way, do you do CBT?" There are variations on this attempt to control a potentially anxious situation but it faces us immediately with the challenge of what to say.

We generally point out that we don't yet know if the person needs treatment or what kind of treatment. "That's why we should spend some time getting to know your story and for you to get to know me. Does that make sense to you?" Most people welcome the opportunity to say something about what's on their mind. This becomes an occasion for the therapist also to begin the transformation from self-help to joint work.

As we listen, questions naturally arise. We listen for whether this is a psychological or medical emergency, mandating that we advise seeking immediate urgent care. Is there something else going on that would be worth investigating before we meet, for instance, a child who needs educational or neuropsychological testing, and so forth?

Usually there is no need for immediate medical intervention or other investigations, but by taking time to speak to the whole person and asking about more than his psychological symptoms we are trying to start a transformation from angry, omnipotent self-sufficiency to the alternative of open-system hope in the healing power of a caring relationship.

We talk about why it's necessary to have an evaluation, so as to develop a set of shared goals and expectations, to start a working relationship, and to address some of the initial expectations. We describe how we will structure the evaluation. As the conversation proceeds, it becomes natural to say, "It seems that there is much we can talk about so let's set up a time when we can meet and think more together about your situation and what will help."

We also request that people write a short note about themselves and send it along before they come to the first appointment. We describe this as "just a page or two of what you think it would be helpful for me to know at the outset" and characterize it as a way to "save you time and money and start me thinking about you."[69]

It is important to be clear about reality at the first call. This too is part of the analyst's open-system stance. We tell people what our fee is, and ask if they can meet that fee. If not, we offer to help them find a lower fee option. We set a date for the initial appointment, tell them about parking and any special directions or arrangements for getting to the office. In all this we are aware that patients inevitably, right from these earliest contacts, transfer their sadomasochistic modes of closed-system defense to the therapeutic situation and relationship, but this can be taken up later. First we are establishing an open-system alternative by being competent, helpful, authoritative, respectful, and realistic.

THERAPEUTIC TASK: INITIATE TRANSFORMATIONS

Transformation starts with the first phone call between strangers meeting and negotiating initial goals. The specific transformations initiated from the outset continue throughout treatment, but are important for the therapist to keep in mind while listening to the earliest communications, as part of assessing both closed- and open-system functioning and the potential for engagement and change.

PATIENT TASK: BRING MATERIAL AND BEGIN TO ENGAGE WITH TRANSFORMATIONS

People are different in their first presentation of themselves. Some people overflow with information and feelings, eager and relieved to be talking with someone who may help. Others are frightened, defensive, reserved, or inhibited, struggling to convey meaningful material, setting up an interview situation, rather than a conversation. How a person responds to the invitation in "How can I help?" or "What brings you to see me at this time?" or "Let's expand on what you conveyed in your note" often intimates a great deal that will become clearer over time about their personality, how they deal with feelings, how they relate to others, and so forth.

Similarly, as the therapist describes some of the transformations they will work on together, valuable information and understanding is conveyed by which ideas make more sense or seem more relevant to the patient, which ones seem painful or aversive, which ones provide a measure of immediate relief.

THERAPIST TASK: EVALUATION SESSIONS – INITIATING TRANSFORMATIONS

Transformation is a real phenomenon throughout life. It's a developmental goal and can fruitfully be used as a barometer of change and open-system functioning throughout treatment. Closed-system functioning is static and repetitive; it interferes with growth, change and transformation. Thus we see a strong link between the two-systems model and attentiveness to transformations at each stage of treatment. All of the following dimensions emerge in some form throughout treatment, but they have particular relevance in the evaluation phase, when patients and therapists are seeking together to determine what is needed and wanted, what strengths are available to help in the effort, how they get on/goodness of fit, and where the areas of difficulty reside.

Self help to joint work: This began in the first phone call, and continues in the first meeting as we engage the client in expanding on the note sent. It feels natural and relaxed to express interest about omissions, or feelings about major life events, information on current family or relationships, knowledge and ideas about their family of origin going back to grandparents and so forth. In this we are modeling another transformation:

Isolated moments to meaningful connections: Our questions can lead the patient to consider the possibility that past and present, outside events and internal processes, trauma and current anxieties, and so forth can have meaningful links and patterns.

We explore the client's symptoms, as we were trained to do and the client expects us to do, but we also ask about strengths, skills, interests, pleasures both currently and in the past. Another way to describe this is that we look at both closed- and open-system functioning, signaling another crucial transformation from:

Focus on pathology to engagement with whole person: This will later be the battle ground for the conflict between closed- and open-system modes of self-regulation. At the evaluation stage it helps to define a goal of treatment as a possible recovery of the joy in past and currently-inhibited open-system sources of self-esteem.

As the client continues to describe symptoms and suffering we listen for how they use closed-system modes to meet basic needs for safety, defense, attachment and gratification. This helps to define another goal of treatment in terms of shifting from predominant use of closed-system defenses to more adaptive open-system coping and responses to challenges. With the patient we can talk about moving from:

Helplessness to competence and ***Despair to hopefulness:*** We talk about how change takes time, effort, patience, manageable steps, pleasure in the process. Many patients carry an unconscious belief in magical solutions. They want therapists to help them restore their magical omnipotence or attribute it to the therapist's magical power and techniques. This is bound to be a major source of resistance and difficulty throughout treatment. We therefore try to start addressing it even in the evaluation. We talk about how together we can find more dependable and satisfying (open-system) ways of meeting their legitimate needs than through (closed-system) suffering. Often this suffering is self-inflicted, leading to looking at:

Guilt to usable concern and ***a tyrannical conscience to a realistic 'inside helper':*** Following relevant material in the evaluation, we may introduce the idea of transforming a harsh, tyrannical super-ego into a realistic and benevolent inside helper to guide, support and encourage. We note instances of harsh judgements and self-condemnation, or times when the person has contravened their own or others' moral standards.

All analysts operate with mental models, as well as attitudes which are overtly or indirectly conveyed to patients. In our clinical work we tend to extend the evaluation period longer than most in order to achieve a genuine, reality-based respect for the patient and a positive conviction that therapy can be effective in providing this person with alternative solutions to past and current anxieties.

We accept that our own models and attitudes will have a profound effect on the patient, especially at the start, and assume that our genuine feeling of hope and confidence is essential to start the process of transformation. Further, by including focus on the patient's areas of open-system functioning, we can create joint treatment goals and start a process that will end in restoring the patient's capacity to choose between alternate systems of self-regulation. This is a dynamic approach to evaluation, in contrast to the nosological approach of the DSM.

RECOMMENDATION

When an evaluation has been extended past one or two initial sessions, we have found that making a recommendation for treatment is much easier. Time has passed, we have come to know each other somewhat and the method of working is familiar. There has usually been some relief and also some positive changes. It is a point where we can engage in deciding with the patient whether we have done enough for now or whether we should start a regular treatment to accomplish more work. What form should that treatment take? What will be most effective, as well as most economical of resources?

There is nothing mystical about frequency. Meeting at greater frequency than once a week makes more time and space for developing the treatment relationship. And, crucially, it allows for practice. Everyone knows and we remind patients that any achievement requires practice. Do they play an instrument, do a sport, know a foreign language? How did they acquire that skill? If they want the changes we have discussed they will have to work, practice, persevere and have the courage to tolerate setbacks and frustration. We convey our confidence that the task is manageable, but of course the commitment is up to the patient.

SETTING THE FRAME – THE WORKING ARRANGEMENTS

Setting the frame and discussing the working arrangements are part of the end of the evaluation phase, once the patient has agreed to engage in a treatment. We have found that there is a series of issues that is often elided, dismissed as merely business, and not as important as the emotional/psychological issues that represent the content of the work. Our experience has been that relegating the business aspects, or "nuts and bolts," to a lesser position general-ly serves defensive needs. If these administrative issues are not

The 'nuts and bolts' matter.

94

realistically addressed in a way that is consistent with forging an open-system, collaborative alliance with patients, the treatment may eventually founder.

In line with the idea of a collaborative relationship and open-system rootedness in reality, we give patients very clear statements of our working arrangements at the stage of making the recommendation for treatment.[70] There is a chance to talk these through at the outset so that no one is surprised. We have found that this establishes an explicit baseline against which we can measure resistance. Most important is that an extended evaluation has established the idea that everything has meaning. Then the working arrangements are not seen only as idiosyncratic whims, but as a way of establishing the importance of the treatment to all parties. We discuss fees, billing practices, responsibility for missed sessions, illnesses, vacations, rescheduling, modes of communication, confidentiality and so forth. We ask for payment to be made at a regular time each month.

THIRTY DAYS' NOTICE

A crucial feature of these discussions is establishing that no changes will be made in the treatment arrangements by *any* party (patient, therapist, parents or child) without thirty days' notice. All therapists have experienced painful summary withdrawals or premature terminations, unilateral announcements of reduction in frequency of sessions, and so forth. By setting up a mutually agreed policy to ensure thirty days to work together before any changes, we have found that many treatments can be saved. The idea of thirty days' notice concretizes the seriousness of the mutual commitment of patient and analyst.

CLINICAL EXAMPLES OF TWO-SYSTEMS TECHNIQUE

EMERGENCE OF OBJECTIVE LOVE

Mr. G was a brilliant scientist with a worldwide reputation in his field, but he was, as he put it, "a selfish, obnoxious pain in the ass,"

95

tyrannical to his wife, children and employees, and seeming to enjoy his sadism without guilt, remorse or conflict. In his first assessment sessions, he described preschool and school-age memories of doing sadistic things to his younger brothers, his mother and his teachers. When he gleefully recounted jumping on a bed until it broke, I chose not to comment on the obviously expressed sadistic triumph, but noted instead the kinesthetic pleasure of jumping up and down.[71] Mr. G was momentarily startled by this response, and then remembered pleasurable school-age experiences of rolling down a grassy slope, with the warm smells of summer and fun with other children.

Mr. G's wife had threatened to leave him unless he sought treatment. He presented a list of abusive behaviors with bravado and a barely concealed challenge to me to reprimand him. Instead, I focused on the essential needs served by his behavior, adding that everyone has these same needs. Mr. G seemed a little flustered by my comment but then recovered by saying that he knows how to get what he needs without asking favors of anyone. I then asked Mr. G. to tell me about his wife. After some initial grumbling about her being unfair, oversensitive and deserving of his abusive behavior he began to talk about her in a softer tone with admiration for her achievements. I said to Mr. G that, despite the fact that he was so hard on his wife, he seemed to value the relationship. Mr. G began to cry and said he felt he couldn't live without her, that he needed treatment in order to keep her.[72]

In the material from Mr. G's evaluation we are struck by the evident excitement and defiance in his sadistic stance. We know from our previous work that the construction of a closed sado-masochistic omnipotent system is a major psychological achievement serving such vital needs as safety, attachment, protection against destruction of self and/or other, sexual discharge and so forth. At this very early time the patient feels the only alternative to closed omnipotent functioning is overwhelming helplessness. In Mr. G's material we see that he has no intention of changing and challenges what he assumes are my intentions.

We attend also to the aspects of open-system functioning. We look for positive pleasures other than sadistic triumph. We look for signs of love, joy, creativity and competence even if these experiences are compromised by closed-system hostile omnipotence. In our model, closed- and open-system responses are available to everyone from birth on, so we expect to find past and current manifestations of open-system functioning, no matter how disturbed the individual. Along these lines we attend to the adaptive dimension of even the most pathological forms of behavior. In the evaluation phase of work with Mr. G. we note that he did look for treatment, that he was aware of the reality of his wife's threats, that there must be sufficient love and positive attachment for him to seek help.[73] Despite the fact that for considerable time Mr. G attributed his success at work, at home and in his numerous affairs to his powerful voice and his bullying, selfish behavior, we also note the high level of success in his field and his pride in his achievements, seeing these as central manifestations of open-system competence.

IDEALIZING ENTHRALLMENT TO JOINT WORK

Mrs. T was a successful businesswoman, married, with three grownup children. She had felt depressed and somewhat empty for a long time, and consulted a psychiatrist, who recommended an antidepressant. Mrs. T was disinclined to use medication, as she felt her friends on pills had lost their zest, even though they claimed to be very happy. She said that she could not decide what to do, so she sought out an analyst, with the idea that he would prescribe analysis. I pointed out that she seemed to have decided that she wanted analysis, but was looking for some expert to take responsibility for the decision. She replied that this was the secret of her success – she had never had to make decisions, but had been pushed throughout her life by circumstances and other people's ideas about her. I wondered about this pattern as a source of difficulty, noting that it implied that she had no wishes of her own, that she had never pursued a desire that could be seen as coming from inside herself. This first verbalization of elements of conflict produced new material. Mrs. T described a number of affairs she had had at conventions in faraway cities and said that she had never told anyone about these before.

I could then discern Mrs. T's conflict over owning her sexual impulses. Rather than interpret at this point on the basis of the content, about which little was yet known, I noted to myself the auguries of erotic transference in this material, and chose first to take up the way Mrs. T seemed to feel that her own wishes could only be met with built-in limits and in secrecy. I suggested that understanding this would be something we could work on together. Mrs. T remarked thoughtfully that she would like to be able to feel good more of the time, not only during those brief, secret affairs, that maybe this problem was what her depression was about. Thus we were able to arrive together at an exploration of her conflicts around pleasure as an explicit goal for her treatment.[74]

Mrs. T's material appears to contrast with Mr. G's. She was aware of suffering, she wanted help and needed no convincing that psychoanalysis was the treatment of choice. She appeared at first glance to be the ideal neurotic patient with a good old-fashioned working alliance and no obvious evidence of closed-system hostile omnipotent sadomasochistic functioning. Working with an internal model of two systems, however, we seek to attend to phenomena in the material that derive from both ways of functioning. Analysts are not always in the habit of thinking of expressed positive wishes for treatment as a possible indicator of conflict and resistance. In this case, I paused mentally to assess the status of the evaluation in the light of the appropriate therapeutic alliance tasks, that is, in relation to the various transformations that should be started before treatment proper begins. Through this lens it became clear that Mrs. T had not begun to shift to the idea of joint work, had not addressed her fantasies around being told what to do by an expert, and was still dealing with her problems as external – we had not yet arrived together at a sense of internal conflict in her. This was the indication that more work was necessary in the evaluation to elucidate her potential for both open- and closed-system functioning.

With Mr. G we looked for manifestations of past and present open-system competent functioning and with Mrs. T we attended more closely to disguised closed-system manifestations. The potential for open- or closed-system responses exists for each person, including the therapist. One clue to Mrs. T's closed-system response to the stress of the evaluation was in my counterreaction. I found myself eager to accept her assessment, to go along with her plan for 5 times per week analysis and to view her notion that we were a good analytic match as based mainly on reality. This rush of positive feelings alerted me to the likelihood that both of us were being swept into a relation of idealizing enthrallment. The two-system model encourages the differentiation of important concepts and phenomena, such as the differences between love in the open and closed systems, or the open- and closed-system determinants in superego development.[75]

With both Mr. G and Mrs. T we attend to open-system functioning as represented in the therapeutic alliance tasks for each phase. Transformation is the task the therapist brings to the evaluation phase; this initiates internal conflict between open- and closed-system functioning. As we have detailed in other publications each open-system therapeutic alliance task challenges a central tenet of the closed system.[76] The closed system is static, movement is illusory and in a closed circle, and change is vigorously resisted. The open system is accessible to internal and external forces; adaptive and creative transformations are the hallmark of this system. Mr. G's defiant sadistic stance was transformed into a source of conflict. Mrs. T's idea that her depression was biological was transformed into an experience of an internal conflict around pleasure. These were the beginning transformations and the basis on which treatment could start.

17

Beginning

THERAPEUTIC TASK: BEING TOGETHER

At the beginning of treatment the patient doesn't know about potential choices of two modes of self-regulation available from birth. This is an idea in the therapist's mind, which gives the therapist a firm stance on the ground of a reality alternative to the borderland the patient has lived in and adapted to. The patient's closed-system modes of self-protection have worked to some extent at earlier times.

PATIENT TASK: BE WITH THE THERAPIST

Now the patient comes to therapy, not to be changed, but usually unconsciously wishing to have the closed system strengthened. The main task of the beginning phase for the patient is to *be with the therapist*. Each patient brings in characteristic ways of feeling safe. This is a general transference, probably visible across many relationships past and present. Although both patient and therapist have worked together and arrived at the decision together, we generally find that the beginning of treatment intensifies anxiety, guilt, conflicts and defenses, offering many examples of characteristic closed-system responses.

"Being with the therapist" seems like a self-evident task for the patient. Yet how one can be with, the conditions one needs to establish to deal with the anxieties one experiences, the way one defends against anticipated loss, betrayal, abandonment and, in general, the multi-determined and multilayered conscious and unconscious layers of *being with* will occupy most of the therapy and are especially prominent at the beginning.

In our field there is an ebb and flow of trends in technical priorities; as we write this book, the emphasis on transference and countertransference is at high tide. We have found that the first transference is usually the transference of defense. These are the unconscious habitual ways the person protects himself from anticipated helplessness. Helplessness is traumatic. What does the patient do in the session and outside to keep from feeling overwhelmed, to feel safe?

Defense analysis as such is not often discussed nowadays, but we see defenses as the main first material that a patient brings into therapy; this is what we work with to strengthen the therapeutic alliance. In various ways we let the patient know that everyone, including ourselves, wants and needs to feel safe and not be overwhelmed. "We're beginning to see what you do here and elsewhere. We won't take that away, but we can look for alternatives which have fewer side effects. Everything has a cost, but, from what you're telling me, you seem to be paying a high price for feeling safe."

Here we may introduce the concept of "emotional muscle" as an alternative to the closed-system, unconscious use of omnipotent defenses. By presenting an alternative open-system mode of self-regulation we are starting the long process of creating an experienced internal conflict between open- and closed-system modes of self-regulation.

THERAPIST TASK: FEEL WITH THE PATIENT

The main task for the therapist in the beginning phase of a treatment is *to feel with the patient*. To "feel with" or "feel into" is a more accurate translation of the German word "Einfuhlung" that Freud used to describe what ana- lysts should do at the beginning of

Empathy includes the whole person.

therapy. The word came originally from art criticism and de- scribed empathy as the capacity to feel into a painting. It was translated by Strachey as "sympathetic understanding" which connotes a more passive listening stance, rather than empathic imagination, which for Freud was an active intellectual process of putting oneself in the place of the other. In our view, sympathy relates mostly to painful experiences, whereas feeling with/empathy includes the whole person both past and present. We have suggested, as have others, that Freud's idea of empathy as "everything an analyst should do ..." is the basis for the idea of a therapeutic alliance and the analyst's active role in starting and maintaining such a pro- cess.[77] Thus when we say "feel with" we mean empathy in its broadest definition. It is not a mystical or a mysterious capacity. It means trying to maintain access to our full store of open-system knowledge, experience, feelings, and imagination.

The model for this attunement is the early mother-child rela- tionship. Fluctuations in attunement may draw on and relate to issues of mother-child attachment during infancy and toddler- hood. We intervene actively when obstacles to being together arise from within the patient, from the environment, or from ourselves. Disruptions and deviations in being with are often our first indi- cators of resistance to engaging in the therapeutic process and direct our attention to describing the conditions under which the patient can be with the therapist.

Typical disruptions take familiar forms, as when patients ex- ternalize their helplessness, confusion, or failure. Not so easy to spot, but part of the same closed, sadomasochistic way of relating, are externalizations of positive ego functions or idealized images of self or other. These can mark periods of heady gratification in the treatment, when therapists can feel terrific. Instead of experi- encing the (open-system) sense of reality-attuned gratification

that comes from doing a good enough job in a difficult and frequently frustrating line of work, the therapist begins to feel like a
long-sought perfect parent/friend/lover. Externalization is a major
defense mechanism in sadomasochistic relationships, and its
operation in the conditions set up by the patient in the treatment
relationship is often signaled by the quality of the analyst's feelings
about the patient and the work.

There are many potential interferences with the analyst's empathy; they often stem from the fact that we have to bear uncertainty,
not knowing, and not being in control of the whole therapeutic
process. The therapist is especially helpless in regard to the patient's willingness and capacity to "be with." Will the patient flee,
withdraw, become enraged before the therapist has any idea why
or whether this is a transference or an error in timing and tact?
The patient comes with years of repetition of closed-system solutions and may become defensively enraged if the omnipotent
solution is undermined. A more likely pattern is to slip covertly
into a secondary defense to protect their omnipotence, such as
phony compliance with treatment (rote recitation of details of
their day or week, for instance), covering up a reinforced omnipotent stance of not changing, not engaging and rendering the
analyst helpless. At the same time they may demand instant results, from an idealized figure they have turned into an
omnipotent savior.

Throughout treatment, open-system experiences may well intensify closed-system defenses at first. The therapist can imagine
what it feels like to use closed-system modes. To yell, force others,
cheat and get away with it, always find the easy way out, be an
exception, break all the rules, and control others by being sadistic
or a victim are powerful and exciting behaviors. There is often
also something very attractive to others in a person who feels and
acts omnipotent. People feel safe and protected by an omnipotent
leader. Patients may cling to omnipotence and/or attribute omnipotence to the therapist, which can be very gratifying. The
therapist may be pulled into feeling safe and protected by the

patient's omnipotence. If the therapy is to move beyond a shared drug high of omnipotence, a closed-system way of being together, both have to become aware of the price paid, to think about therapy as a means to an end, rather than an end in itself, and be able to imagine the possibilities of a rich and creative life after therapy.

When the therapist verbalizes some of the obstacles to being with, the patients can at times feel enormous relief and the intense adaptive gratification of communicating and being listened to. These feelings are both a major goal and a result of the beginning phase, and the experience becomes a powerful positive motive for the therapeutic alliance. It is not something brought to treatment by the patient, nor is it supplied by an omnipotent therapist. Indeed, omnipotent externalization and attunement are inversely related.

Attunement is created by both patient and therapist out of the effort to note together the difficulties in the alliance task of being with the therapist, whether the obstacles come from within the patient, from the environment, or from the therapist. The experience of attunement, which taps into and reverberates with powerful feelings from our earliest relationships, is a genuine source of positive feelings. We allocate this experience to open-system functioning. Reality-based love between individuals grows out of sharing the satisfaction of these ego needs. The moments of attunement that result from the work of the beginning phase are the building blocks of objective love between therapist and patient.

SIGNIFICANT OTHER/PARENT TASK: ALLOW PATIENT TO BE WITH ANOTHER

An often-neglected factor deserves mention here. That is the therapeutic task for the significant other of an adult patient or the parents of a child or adolescent patient. The task for the significant other is to *allow the patient to be with another* person. We know from child and adolescent work that insufficient attention to the reactions of parents is the major cause of treatment failure.

This should alert us to the reality that adults' partners are also likely to have reactions to the patient entering into a long, private, expensive, and time-consuming relationship with an unknown person. Imagine what it feels like to have one's spouse or partner enter into therapy and not be able or willing to share what is being said to this stranger. The partner or parent may feel the threat of loss of the patient, or loss of their love, giving rise to self-protective defensive reactions of withdrawal or externalization.

The therapist must be mindful of whether the patient has turned the privacy of the treatment situation into closed-system hostile secrecy.[78] Has the patient turned the therapist into an unwitting accomplice to an abusive action? If not attended to, the real impact on the significant other may lead to a subtle but powerful battle with the therapist for the love and attention of the patient. The patient may intensify feelings of being excluded, leading to destructive jealousy in the partner. Since the patient may relish the idea of people fighting over him, the therapist may not know what is going on until it's too late. Equally frequent is the pattern where a patient shares every private thought with a partner and creates what we have called a "negative therapeutic alliance," designed to cement a fragile relationship by externalizing blame and failure on to the therapist.[79] A simple comment, such as "you haven't mentioned your wife's reaction to you starting therapy," may keep these issues included in the therapeutic work.

CLINICAL EXAMPLES OF TWO-SYSTEMS TECHNIQUE

CLOSED-SYSTEM BEING WITH

19-year-old Nick had come for an evaluation because he found university an extremely painful experience even though he had little difficulty handling the academic demands. He was the second of three children in a middle-class family. Nick's infancy and preschool years sounded unremarkable. There were apparently no potentially traumatic events such as major medical interventions or losses and so forth. Through school he had few friends, no girlfriends, and seemed tortured by guilt and despair. He felt that he had wasted his whole adolescence on drugs and alcohol, had not learned any social skills and had no idea what he wanted to do with the rest of his life. He felt lost, confused and in pain. Nick ended up in late adolescence with an omnipotent belief in suicide as his solution to his difficulties.

As he settled into 4 times per week treatment, he frequently became silent, would grimace as if he were in physical pain, squirmed and twisted on the couch, and beat it with his fist, all with no apparent reason and no discernible precipitant. I was puzzled and confused and also found it uncomfortable to be with him. This behavior went on for a while. Along with registering developmental images, such as we have described in our earlier chapter on infancy, I found myself thinking about how we had found in our original study of beating fantasies in children that all the therapists reported discomfort in being with their patients. I said that I was getting a sense that he might have experienced a very painful, confusing and frustrating experience with his mother during infancy. I wondered if I were currently being made to feel what he had felt as an infant.

Soon after, Nick told his mother what I had said. His mother did not respond directly, but walked out of the room. She later wrote a letter to him. She told him that, when he was a baby, she had felt unable to hold him, hug him or tell him that she loved him. She had cared for his physical needs, but then left him in his crib to cry himself to sleep. Nick's mother was the eldest child with a brother 3 years younger. In the mother's memory, her brother was adored, much loved and preferred. In the course of Nick's treatment we could explore together the probability that Nick represented the hated male rival who left her feeling abandoned and depressed.

FEELING SAFE

Ms. J, an older woman highly esteemed in her demanding field, came to analysis because of a crippling depression and a badly-ended previous therapy. From the beginning, she made me the center of her universe, thinking constantly of my voice, my expressions, my activities, how I might react to what she was doing or not doing and so forth. In sessions for the first few months, she literally cast herself at my feet, curling up under the blanket on the floor in front of my chair. Alternately nesting and hiding, she wanted me to change her, to lift her out of despair and tell her how to move forward again.

This intense investment and extreme-looking presentation might have alarmed me. I did not yet know much about her history, beyond her many attempts at therapy, but I registered inside that I felt relatively comfortable keeping her company for the time being in this state. When I wonder about this, looking back, I think my initial calm was directly related to experience working with children and adolescents. They don't come in, lie on the couch and try to free associate. Their material comes in many forms – the how is interesting and needs to be analyzed as well, but it isn't so important right away.

The patient's task at the beginning is to be with the therapist. Ms. J was able to be with me under the conditions she created. That enabled me to feel with her. As long as we were both safe, a prime consideration when dealing with the many ways children bring themselves and their material to treatment, I felt all right with joining her where she was in the conditions she had to set up to be together. Much later in the treatment we could return to this unusual way of being with and discover that it related to being cared for and having her needs met by the nurses during a long hospital stay for a serious illness in early childhood.

IMPACT OF SADOMASOCHISTIC TRANSFERENCE

A very accomplished middle-aged man had spent many years in psychotherapy with another clinician, but came to me for consultation when old symptoms recurred. Mr. H felt he had been trapped with his earlier therapist and that no movement had taken place for years. Although the work they had done on his early relationship with a very disturbed mother had been useful to him, he was terrified of resuming any therapy, as he had found his deep regression overwhelming and feared the unbearable pain of inevitable separations.

During the evaluation he had reacted with intense feeling to even minor interventions, and had found it almost impossible to take anything in when he began to feel too much. When treatment began, Mr. H talked a lot, jumping from subject to subject. Sometimes he told me not to speak, because he could not listen. A controlling atmosphere, created by the threat of his extreme emotions, began to set in. I alternated between being annoyed and worrying that the patient might be more disturbed than he had initially appeared.

Mr. H's emotional controlling created a barrier to progress and a pressure for a relationship ruled by intense, primitive affects. If I felt with him solely on the level that he sought to be on with me, there would be a connection between us, but it would be one based only on shared pain. This would reenact the traumatic undifferentiated relationship with his mother that had been repeated in the earlier treatment. If I retreated from contact with Mr. H's deep feelings, there was a risk of treatment failure through lack of imagination and affective resonance.

I reminded myself that the therapeutic task includes feeling with the whole person of the patient, not only relating to his closed-system functioning, but also staying in touch with the knowledge I carried of Mr. H's open-system capacities at many different levels. I could contain my potential to react with hostility or vindictive withdrawal from Mr. H's controlling presentation of only one aspect of his personality by holding on to the progressive goal of relating to Mr. H as a real, separate, whole person with many different feelings and skills. Mr. H responded to the steadiness of my regard with a gradual expansion of his emotional range and repertoire, as he found new ways to be with me and participate in the work of the treatment.

THE POWER OF CLOSED-SYSTEM SOLUTIONS
AND GENERATING CONTRAST

Mr. F started his analysis by talking about his battles at work and his impulse to argue with me about anything and everything, especially about the vacation schedule. He described growing up in a home where the men were, as he put it, "sadistic bullies" who dominated and brutalized the women. As his history unfolded and was re-experienced in the transference, he began to see clearly the relation between feelings of helpless anxiety when he was little and his reaction of identification with his shouting, verbally abusive father.

When he was angry, he felt a rush, an excitement, a feeling of power and indestructibility. Mr. F gave many examples of acting recklessly in states of anger and made it clear that he attributed all of his many achievements to never holding back his rageful, bullying behavior. He thought his voice was overwhelmingly powerful and that he could get anything he wanted by shouting.

While hearing about and often being the target of Mr. F's attacks, I also tracked his good feelings in the sessions, noting when he seemed to enjoy coming and using his mind. There were days when we could see he felt good being listened to, understood and respected. Little by little we began to talk about how important these ordinary, legitimate human needs really are. Mr. F recaptured early memories of his grandmother who had loved him and treated him as a worthy individual. Alongside treating me either as the threatening father of his childhood or as the carrier of externalized helpless and denigrated parts of himself, he also began to relate to me as someone more like his grandmother. He recovered a loving, joyful aspect of himself, an open-system way of being, in distinct contrast to his closed-system image and experience of himself as omnipotently magical and destructive.

The omnipotent defenses made him feel safe and powerful; his love left him feeling vulnerable, especially to abandonment. Focus on his feelings around being with me allowed for repeated experiences of his conflict between two ways of functioning. There was a gradual expansion of pleasure from competence in his external life, particularly at work, where his organizational and research activities were notably successful. Mr. F began to comment on how good that felt.

The closed-system sadomasochism enacted in Mr. F's provocative argumentativeness had become largely restricted to hostile interactions at home with his wife, and, more subtly, with his older child. He usually mentioned these battles with his wife in passing, always with self-justifying evidence, and never really stayed with the issues. I continued to listen, trying to feel with Mr. F's desperate need to keep himself in a dominant position, but I also remarked whenever possible on the contrast between the two sets of feelings, wondering out loud about what he thought would actually happen if he didn't bluster and bellow.

One day, Mr. F mused out loud "I wonder if I really need to be such a bully all the time, especially with my kid?" This spark of curiosity represented a significant shift into a more realistic open-system stance of looking at himself. Mr. F began to question his own need to stay "locked into this provocative stuff," and laughed ruefully when he said "I do it with you all the time, don't I?" Sessions began to feel very different, as Mr. F began to relax into feeling safe without fighting all the time. He had come through to bringing his open-system capacities into play in the collaborative work.

FACING CONFLICT BETWEEN TWO SYSTEMS

Mrs. T, whom we first met in the chapter on the evaluation phase, attended regularly and punctually when she began her treatment, reporting in conscientious detail the events of her life. But a pattern began to emerge in which she presented material and left it to me to make something of it. My occasional remarks (for instance, about Mrs. T's relationships with fellow workers) were accepted, but Mrs. T never seemed to take them further. In the beginning phase of treatment, the patient's therapeutic task is to be with the analyst; the analyst strives to feel with the patient.

With these tasks in mind, I began to understand her apparent compliant passivity as her way of being with me. Mrs. T's conditions for feeling safe in the relationship included externalizing her ego capacities for reflection and integration onto me to create a sadomasochistic transference that cast her in the role of a naive child sitting at the feet of a wise elder. As the images in her material brought this relationship into sharper focus, I pointed out how rarely Mrs. T seemed comfortable with the idea that we were two adults working together—that is, I interpreted the closed-system interference with the open-system task.

Mrs. T exclaimed, "Why come at all if you won't do it?" She said that she was sure that she could eventually force me to take care of her and decide everything for her if she only waited it out and did as she was told. This harked back to her initial push to have an expert tell her what was wrong with her and what she should do about it. I had used the therapeutic task of being with another as a lens to help myself see more clearly the dimensions of the sadomasochistic transference as it was emerging; when I took this up with Mrs. T, her underlying omnipotent belief in being able to find a way to control me emerged and became accessible to the work of the analysis.

Together we began to explore why she needed to establish this way of being with me. At first this effort produced moments of rage and panic in Mrs. T. She reported staying awake at night, feeling unable to think whenever she tried to imagine herself as my equal and resenting my demands on her. "I don't know what makes you think I can do any of this," she snapped, "and what would really happen if I did? What would you really feel?" Mrs. T's fear of my reaction led to memories of her mother, a person of low intelligence who had barely finished grade school. Depressed throughout Mrs. T's childhood, she had always become extremely defensive whenever Mrs. T won a school prize, demonstrated any competence at home, or simply looked attractive. Through the lens of the task of being with me, Mrs. T's conflicts over trusting that it could be safe to be herself in a relationship were illuminated and brought explicitly into the relationship with me. With continued attention to how Mrs. T externalized her open-system ego functions, she gradually became more involved in the analytic work, making spontaneous observations and at times associating to her dreams without prompting. The workings of her own mind were gradually becoming an object of her curiosity. This marked her transition into the middle phase of the treatment.

The first part of this book summarizes closed- and open-system modes of self-regulation in response to the challenges of development through the phases of life. Familiarity with the changing repertoire of closed-system solutions may help therapists put themselves in the patient's shoes. Then they can begin to explore together what patients are protecting themselves from and what legitimate needs are being met by their adult version of an infantile attachment through pain, a toddler tantrum and belief that ordinary assertion is aggressive, the preschool linking of sexual excitement to sadism, the school age avoidance of work, the adolescent consolidation of the omnipotent belief that others can be controlled through sadomasochistic behavior. The development section also describes potential open-system responses to meet the same legitimate needs for safety, attachment, self protection, gratification and purpose.

We are suggesting that, starting from the very first contact, through the evaluation and recommendation, and into the beginning phase of treatment the idea of an alternate mode of self-regulation has been modeled and introduced. If both therapist and patient can see omnipotence in action, begin to see its destructive effects and are willing to do the work to set aside the patient's dependence and addiction to closed-system functioning, then therapy can move into the long middle phase to work on open-system alternatives.

18

Middle

THERAPEUTIC TASK: WORKING TOGETHER

In the first part of this book we described analysis as a developmental experience. As such, it has a goal and direction. But we don't characterize treatment only as a linear progression along a path from pathology to health. Rather, we see treatment as involving work on both closed- and open-system potentials operating throughout in patients and therapists. Both aspects have to be addressed in each phase of treatment.

The closed system operates, as one patient put it, "like a hamster wheel – a lot of noise, but it goes nowhere." The open system is responsive to reality and is constantly changing. In the detailed example of Mrs. T at the end of the last chapter we saw her internal pressure to remain in an idealized relationship that had become safe and familiar for her. She wanted to stay with her analyst as the wise elder who was empathic, had insights and answers to her conflicts, and could rescue her from all of life's difficulties. That would keep her in a childlike state, a pitiable victim absolved from guilt or responsibility for her predicament. From the side of the therapist, we can see that it could seem both easier and more gratifying to remain idealized and stay involved in the cyclical loop of Mrs. T's habitual ways of regulating her feelings and relationships. The therapy can stalemate without a focus on and shift to the issue of joint work and what gets in the way of it.

This is a frequent pattern that patients seek to establish and maintain in therapeutic relationships, transferring old, practiced ways of being with others to the new setting of treatment. Analysts are inevitably drawn into such patterns, both by empathic role-responsiveness and by the closed-system potential in everyone. This is where we find support and technical enhancement in thinking in two-systems terms. When we remember that treatment has a direction, that the goal is to offer the patient ways to have authentic freedom to choose how to respond to life's challenges, then we can keep one foot in open-system reality. Throughout the evaluation and the beginning phases, while listening to, understanding, verbalizing, and interpreting the patient's closed-system functioning, we also notice, describe, remind, and underscore instances of open-system activity and satisfaction. Over time, as we saw with all the patients described in the last chapter, as with Mrs. T, the contrast between closed- and open-system solutions becomes noticeable.

We have found that thinking about and working with the open-system capacities that every patient has, no matter how disturbed they are, allows for the emergence of an alternative positive cycle, in contrast to the vicious cycles of closed-system functioning. The work of the middle phase facilitates the emergence of open-system functioning, so that the patient can experience an internal conflict between the two systems of self-regulation. The experience of this conflict provides patients with a genuine choice for sources of satisfaction, the incentives of dependability and agency to set aside closed-system solutions and gratifications and discover, even if fleetingly at first, that the open system offers more reliable and genuine pleasures at lower cost. The therapist too appreciates the pleasure of functioning at peak efficiency and values the person with whom that can be done. The sense of each as a separate person is integral to developing objective or realistic love and admiration for the other. Conflict between the two systems shows in the areas of relationships, work, and feelings.

PATIENT TASK: WORKING TOGETHER WITH THERAPIST

The therapeutic alliance task of the middle phase is *working together*. Working together is, however, a mixed experience that brings great satisfaction in the process and achievement of understanding, but also carries with it inevitable disappointments at limitations in insight, difficulties in communication, and transient dyssynchronies between patient and analyst. This task of the therapeutic alliance stands in direct contradiction to the delusional image of perfect communion so fundamental to closed-system omnipotent denial of separateness.

Conflicts about working together can be intense. Patients are deeply invested and loyal to closed-system solutions because they feel familiar and safe; they represent attachments and connections to primary people in the patient's life and history; they organize experience; they structure relationships. The therapeutic alliance task of working together creates an open-system relationship in the treatment that challenges all these functions of closed-system ways of living.

One crucial distinction between the open and closed systems of self-regulation is the relation to work. In the closed system work is not only avoided, but is experienced as a threat to the omnipotent belief that things can and should be achieved from wishing and forcing, rather than working. This magical notion is reinforced by a society in which hard work has developed a bad reputation. Most people think that easy is desirable. This seems to hold in our general culture and even in our own field, where pressures for quick and easy fixes come from insurance carriers, pharmaceutical companies, patients, and our own omnipotent wishes. Rollo May, an important eclectic American analyst, is said to have remarked that patients may be willing to put their backs on the couch, but avoid putting their shoulders to the wheel. Thus the middle phase, with its emphasis on work and the obstacles that arise to accomplishing and enjoying it, is central in multiple ways and demands significant time and emotional investment.

Working effectively together can provide deep satisfaction. Both people can experience open-system gratification and dependable fueling of positive self-esteem from shared experiences of collaboration, competence, pleasure in the process, and the joy of creativity. This is very different from sadomasochistic pleasure from ideas of omnipotent control of others. The contrast between pleasure in competent functioning and closed-system excitement from the illusory gains of sadomasochistic triumph becomes a powerful perception that relates to the difference between self-regard based on realistic progressive achievements and skills, and self-regard based on an economy of pain and aggression.[80] Working together in the treatment relationship is a new source of open-system pleasure that provides a base for the elaboration of realistic capacities that provide a viable alternative to old closed-system sources of good feelings about the self. Reality-oriented satisfaction motivates further collaborative work. Repeated experience of pleasure from competence and creativity is necessary to a patient's developing a conflict between different ways of self-regulation.

For adults the middle phase of treatment can be an opportunity to rework schoolage tasks and conflicts. The challenges of middle childhood to negotiate rules, rewards, demands, and controls of the external world, to find ways to enjoy work, sharing, and taking turns, to appreciate the separateness and individuality of others, rather than using them as objects for externalizing – all these appear in adult forms in the material of the middle phase of treatment. The style, tone, and functioning of conscience resonates with childhood potential for closed-system perfectionism, a crippling omnipotent belief that can pervade and undermine all adult functioning.

In the middle phase, treatment provides a space where patients can play and so safely explore their thoughts, feelings, and desires. Working together, with the competent exercise of ego functions, provides an experience of good mental functioning, satisfies deep ego needs for both patient and analyst, and draws on the accumulated transformations of early experiences of attunement, self-regulation and adaptive pleasure. It motivates further work and aids the internalization of collaboration. This internalization allows for interior dialogue and exploration in patient and therapist, and nourishes creativity, with its accompanying feelings of joy. Part of working together is acknowledgment of this pleasure. If the patient or the therapist does not feel the joy of creativity or cannot share it, this failure signals inhibition of ego functioning and can be used as an entry point for exploring underlying conflicts around feeling good, for thinking together about what impedes open-system pleasure in real achievements and creative experiences.

Patients may react to all of the conflicts and challenges described above with repeated reversion to characteristic externalizing defenses. Externalization is a major defense mechanism in closed-system functioning. It is a manifestation of what we and others have called "soul blindness," an abusive denial of the real individuality of others.[81] Sometimes there are frank projections of impulses, but, most often, we see externalizations of disowned, shameful, or denigrated aspects of the self, with the person using the analyst or others as carriers. When the major conflicts involve experiences of success or pleasure, when the person unconsciously equates achievement with aggression, attack, damage, or murder, positive capacities or ego functions may be attributed to the analyst. As treatment proceeds, instances of externalization usually decrease, but may persist in ever more subtle manifestations, in tone of voice, casually-reported remarks to others, word choice, or rationalized ordinary incidents.

THERAPIST TASK: MAXIMUM USE OF EGO FUNCTIONS

During the middle phase, variations in the analyst's ego functioning and associated feelings can also be used to track the pattern of the therapeutic relationship. Whether these are characterized as either counter-reactions and countertransferences, or subsumed under the general heading of countertransferences, they are an important source of information and a barometer of the state and progress of the treatment. Therapists can be alive to feelings of quiet, sustained pleasure in joint work, joy and admiration in seeing the patient's flowering capacity for creative insight, boredom and distraction when the patient withdraws into an omnipotent pseudoindependent stance, and the mixture of gratification and discomfort when the patient externalizes ego functions and idealizes the analyst.

Work in the middle phase can be long, painful and often frustrating to the therapist, as the patient clings to the closed system and tries to provoke the analyst to act in a way that pushes the patient into what Steiner called a "psychic retreat."[82] We have pointed out that an omnipotent delusion cannot be maintained without the participation of the external world.[83] Our own feelings and conscious and unconscious responses are part of the patient's external reality. Patients may retreat from the risks of realistic functioning for their own internal reasons, but if this reaction is too frequent or too prolonged, we have to examine ourselves to see if we are contributing to the difficulty. We might be reacting to the patient's new pleasure and creativity with envy; we may be reacting to the patient's growing self-analytic competence with feelings of rejection, uselessness, or loss; the thought of impending termination may evoke worries ranging from loss of income to fears of abandonment and depression.

If we cannot work through such feelings, the patient, perhaps in repetition of earlier childhood experiences, may feel unable to sustain a sense of "true self."[84] The true self encompasses the capacities of the open system, while a "false self" is part of a defensive construction striving for an omnipotent capacity to care for and control a depressed or unavailable, abusive, or lost parent. If we can work through our own psychic retreat from conflicts about the patient's progression, we can help the patient consolidate the possibility of open-system self-regulation and move forward from the static timelessness of omnipotent beliefs.

The middle phase brings a risk of premature termination. The work of the middle phase has brought the open system into play. In contrast to the timeless, unrealistic universe of the closed system, the open system is rooted in the reality of change. Issues of change, progression, loss, sadness, and mortality are inevitably present. The pull to closed-system denial of the realities of generation and time is strong. Resistance can take many forms, from conscious refusal to think about the future, to denial of changes already accomplished, to unconscious maintenance of more subtle forms of pathological patterns, to flights to medication or alternative therapies, or precipitating a unilateral premature termination. Leaving treatment precipitately often repeats closed-system patterns of separation in adolescence.

Steady work on the pleasures and benefits of working together counters the pull of magical solutions and strengthens the patient's sense of competence and mastery. Additionally, the therapist has to *Working together in the middle phase is practice for living and self-analysis.* trust that the patient will eventually regain full access to his or her optimal capacities. The new level and range of ego functions used to *work together* in alliance with the analyst throughout the middle of analysis can be used for living and for self-analysis. In addition to ego functions such as memory, perception, self-reflection, integration and so forth are the metacognitive functions that Freud referred to as the executive function of the ego, and that Anna Freud described as the general characteristics of the personality. Included here would be the capacity to plan, anticipate, work through a task from beginning to completion, take pleasure in the process and so forth.

During the middle phase the therapist too may experience a conflict between the two systems, between the rush of omnipotent gratification and the less intense but more genuine and sustained good feeling of reality-based regard for the patient and for oneself in relation to the patient. It is in connection with the middle-phase pleasures of working together that we find new relevance in our idea of two systems of self-regulation and can use it to evolve criteria to differentiate a relationship that is exploitative from one that is beneficial and mutually enhancing.

By the middle phase there have been big changes in the relationship between patient and therapist. The time spent together, the safety and reliability of the setting and the analyst, the shared understanding of details of the patient's current life and history, patients' emotional relief at being listened to and validated – all contribute to a stronger, more realistically caring and respectful relationship. This is the context that makes the hard work of the middle phase possible; it provides a container, a safety net and cushion for painful, hard-won insights, the patient's internal struggles, and the inevitable friction and tension that will arise between patient and therapist as they grapple with conflict between different ways of self-regulation.

Therapists can feel confident that patients have a strong enough positive, open-system relationship to them and the treatment, that defenses are less brittle and monolithic, that enough alternative coping strategies have been developed for them to be able to hear upsetting or painful interventions that confront old patterns of closed-system functioning. The patient's recourse to closed-system modes can often arouse frustration and anger in the therapist, who may then shift into a scolding, directive, sadistic superego mode. It sometimes helps the therapist to remember that habitual closed-system functioning, as a source of sadomasochistic gratification, leads to physiological changes as well as psychological habits. Those changes become a powerful addiction, involving the same endogenous opioids as drugs or alcohol. Here too a two-systems model helps us consider that addictions can only be substantively addressed when patients have alternative solutions available. From a psychological vantage point, the open-system alternative offers a safer, less costly and pleasurable alternative.

SIGNIFICANT OTHERS/PARENTS TASK: ALLOW FOR PSYCHOLOGICAL SEPARATENESS

As noted earlier, patients' partners and the parents of child and adolescent patients play crucial dynamic roles in the unfolding and often the fate of the therapeutic relationship. Even if they are not a practical part of the treatment setting, we have to be mindful of their presence, needs, feelings, and effects on patients. The transition to the middle phase of treatment can be difficult for significant others or parents because the patient now has a different investment in the work and the analyst, which includes not only transference feelings and defensive externalizations, but also regard for the therapist as a separate person with whom there is valued, pleasurable shared experience. Partners or parents may feel lonely, left out, or rivalrous, and may react to protect their familiar character defenses and their version of past history.[85] These are challenges that patients and therapists can meet with either closed- or open-system responses, that also relate to the presence and operation of a closed- or open-system conscience.[86] Closed-system functioning is often embedded in a pathological equilibrium within a family or a couple. Change and growth in open-system functioning can disrupt that balance and reveal that the patient is changing at a different rate than the others.

CLINICAL EXAMPLES OF TWO-SYSTEMS TECHNIQUE

AFFECTIVE RESONANCES OF CONFLICT BETWEEN TWO SYSTEMS

Nick, whom we first met in the chapter on the beginning phase, struggled with the task of *working together* in the middle phase, as it challenged his omnipotent belief that others would be beaten, threatened or destroyed by his achievements. His protection was to do things alone and in secret. As the work proceeded I commented on the times we worked well, when together we accomplished more than either alone. I pointed out the reality that his good work did not threaten or hurt me, and, most importantly, noted explicitly when the work together was pleasurable. Initially those open-system moments were almost non-existent or were so fleeting that they could easily pass unremarked. When we spotted the operation of an omnipotent belief, we traced it developmentally, reconstructing each phase in the evolution of his closed-system responses. This process brings the underlying unconscious magical assumptions into the ego to be explored. My developmental knowledge provided a safely displaced, neutral context in which Nick could feel understood, and could experience my empathy. Here analysts can be teachers who have the knowledge and experience to speak with authority.

Noting the pleasure of cooperative work led to Nick's obvious anxiety in feeling good. He would slip back into silence or inhibition; we could then focus on his conflict over ordinary good feelings. This was a new conflict, one clearly between closed-system sadistic triumph and open-system mutual pleasure. "This is nuts" he said, "feeling good makes me feel scared!" It also made him feel lonely and sad, realizing how much he missed not having anyone to share things with, how it kept him alone. This work then helped him to take an opportunity to collaborate with a retired scientist. Together they created an innovative and much-used virtual computer program. "I guess Prof. is the father I never had. I still find myself thinking he'll be upset at something I figure out but in fact he's delighted. It's like you said, most people enjoy doing things together."

We did extensive work on Nick's rage at women and his omnipotent defenses against feeling helpless to get what he needed from his mother. It is clinically important to acknowledge and verbalize the intense experience of anger. We address this as an unfinished task from toddlerhood, when parents should ordinarily help the child master feelings and transform feeling-states into useful signal affect. Patients of all ages respond well to reconstruction of such failure in early interactions, recognizing the dynamic and often feeling strong empathy and sympathy for their younger selves.

This work had enabled him to start going out with women, but he always managed to do something to have them disappoint him; then he could reject them. He felt relieved when each relationship ended. We talked about his belief that he had to be invulnerable, never to be surprised by a rejection. He could always be in charge and make it happen. I agreed that being alone is a powerful protection, but then reminded him of the pleasure he had in doing things together. Perhaps he could work to build up the emotional muscle to tolerate sadness and rejection.[87] We could use the experiences of separation in our relationship to exercise those muscles and practice making distinctions among rejections, losses and ordinary absences. Some time later Nick had a relationship that ended when the woman went back to her old boyfriend. "It is sad, I feel hurt," he said, "but it's not the end of the world. I'm still me and I'll keep going. I don't quit tennis when I lose a match, why should I quit going out. It's better than convincing myself that I don't need anyone but really being very lonely."

EMOTIONAL STATES TO SIGNAL AFFECT;
DIFFERENCE BETWEEN ASSERTION AND AGGRESSION

Mr. M was a highly successful businessman, who felt proud of having powered his way through challenges and obstacles to become a multi-millionaire. He told me that, when facing a potential business challenge, he would pump himself up into a rage by saying, "that bastard will take food from my children's mouths if I let him. I'll kill him first." He regarded this as the secret of his success. He had been a semi-pro hockey player; for a number of years he had coached local youth teams until he was banned for repeatedly threatening referees.

The work with Mr. M illustrates the distinction we draw between a closed-system emotional state and open-system signal affects. He struggled to manage and maintain his constant state of rage, in contrast to a signal of anger that would give him access to open-system assertion. Arrested after a belligerent incident, Mr. M was ordered by the court to see me for anger management and his first panicky thought was that I would take his anger away. He spent much of the beginning phase challenging and trying to provoke me – assuming I was a 'bleeding-heart liberal,' he laughingly spewed extreme right-wing Fox News 'facts' at me. He was bringing in his characteristic way of relating, creating the only kind of conditions that made him feel safe.

I told him that anger was a crucially useful feeling, as it tells us what we like and don't like. Our discussion continued over time, as I said our aim was not to take his anger away, but to find ways to make it an effective tool that could work for him, rather than against him. I noted that it takes muscle and self-discipline to use anger as a signal to activate his mind, so that he could problem-solve and become assertive. Little kids and idiots fly into a rage, but aggression and assertion are different.

In our work on emotional muscle we describe how parents have to differentiate assertion and aggression and help their children learn the same distinction. The focus on this muscle in the four-year-old year builds on earlier practice of naming feelings, making feelings just the right size, and using anger as a signal. Mr. M had no specific trauma at two or four. What he suffered in childhood was the blanket imposition of his mother's pervasive, smothering anxiety about his father, who travelled a lot on business. She worried constantly that he would die. Mr. M spent as much time as possible out of the house; his athletic skills became a way to fight off and avoid being caught in the fog of his mother's panic. Every step forward felt like an aggressive triumph over this drag, rather than an assertive achievement to be enjoyed and celebrated, and used as a stepping-stone to the next.

Including this open-system focus on the emotional muscle of bolstering his assertion with the rest of the usual therapeutic attention to his closed-system transferences and defenses addressed his neurotic conflicts and allowed his progressive development to resume. Two years later, Mr. M was reinstated as coach of a local high school hockey team. He took them to the state championships. He told his players that he had learned from a psychologist the difference between assertion and aggression and the strength it takes to maintain that distinction. "When the other team plays dirty," he said, "I don't want you to retaliate with stupid aggression. I want you to be twice as assertive – skate twice as fast, work twice as hard and shoot twice as much!"

CLOSED- AND OPEN-SYSTEM SUPEREGOS IN CONFLICT

During the beginning phase of Mr. Z's treatment we explored his need to "beat himself up," focusing on the actuality of moments of pleasure that he had difficulty bringing in to his treatment. This expansion of technique to include listening for and attending to areas of experience that seem outside of pathology stems directly from our two-system conceptualization of self-regulation. Often this interest is reacted to with surprise, as when Mr. Z said with scorn and sarcasm, "I thought you were getting paid, vast sums I may add, to listen to my misery, not my pleasures!" Gradually, however, there were periods of good feeling when he could experience feelings of self-worth and competence. He began to notice the oscillation between his superego condemnation of himself and his superego permission for pleasure. This led to explication of some past and current determinants in the formation and persistence of his harsh, sadomasochistic superego. Noteworthy was the relation between self-condemnation and separation. On return from a vacation, putting himself down became a way to reconnect: "If I feel good, what reason do I have for returning?"

Mr. Z began to realize there was an alternative to his automatic self-condemnation. His difficulty in assuming that he and I could simply feel good being together became the focus. At first Mr. Z attributed this problem to his bad relationship with his father, idealizing his mother, but it soon became apparent that his early relationship with his mother was very burdened. She was overstressed during her husband's frequent protracted absences on business and struggled to pay consistent attention to him. Mr. Z's father was largely absent for most of the first four years of his life, and his mother relied on him as the little "man of the house." Overstimulating physical closeness alternated with withdrawal and abandonment whenever his father returned. A painful relationship between ego and superego helped Mr. Z maintain an internal connection with both his parents and all subsequent parental objects, including his analyst.

When he was a schoolboy, Mr. Z's relationship with his father deteriorated further. He responded to his father's criticism by isolating himself and spending his time dreaming of superheroes. An important technical turn in the work came with shared conviction around the reconstruction that Mr. Z had "chosen" to disappoint his father, to get a B instead of an A, to miss the clear shot on goal. Mr. Z's masochistic presentation activated his father's sadistic attacks and made father a villain in mother's eyes. This perpetuated Mr. Z's omnipotent belief in his oedipal victory over the wicked absent father.

In treatment this first emerged in his externalization of sadism on to me, which made Mr. Z into the special, entitled victim. This was his way of perpetuating the vicious closed cycle, in which his omnipotent self-image led to maintaining a conscience that had to be draconian to control the omnipotent impulses.[88] As we were able to make open-system realistic reconstructions[89] of the evolution and functions of this closed cycle, the technical focus shifted from Mr. Z as passive victim to active constructor of his personality in order to explore his *choice* of maintaining closed-system functioning, rather than developing the expanded possibilities for good feeling and rootedness in reality of the open system, despite what he experienced as its attendant risks.

As the middle phase proceeded, we were able to explore another layer in Mr. Z's omnipotent belief system. On the surface he seemed so respectable, law-abiding, religious, and moral, engaged in a host of "good works," respected by all. But he had no pleasure or pride in accomplishments: in treatment he often "forgot" to mention honors and awards, or the loving actions of his children and grandchildren.

He said that talking of those would be bragging and he could not think of anything worse. He tortured himself with thoughts of imperfection in his work and imagined infidelity by his wife in the past and after his death. At the same time, he sneaked off to massage parlors and later became addicted to internet pornography. He searched out adult mentors and then seduced them sexually. All this was done under unbearably intense physical and psychological pressure to action, a compulsion "to do something and do it quickly." This helped us to further explore and understand the pull of guaranteed gratification in closed-system sadomasochistic activities, whatever the costs or dangers.

Mr. Z's pressure on himself and the analyst to find an immediate solution became a theme for a long period of the middle phase. The lack of a quick, easy solution was recognized as a source of intense disappointment in himself, the analyst, and the analytic process. Mr. Z found temporary relief in joyless and potentially dangerous homosexual cruising, driving drunk, and staying up all night before an important meeting surfing pornographic internet sites with special interest in bondage and sadomasochistic sexual encounters. This secret omnipotent behavior finally receded when it was identified as an addiction to closed-system solutions to anxiety and conflict, an excited sexual rush that worked for Mr. Z to meet vital needs from many levels. We have noted earlier that closed-system omnipotent resolution of oedipal conflicts puts the stamp of "quick and easy" on all subsequent responses to conflicts, obstacles, and challenges.[90] The middle phase tasks of working together throw such issues into sharp relief.

FEELINGS AND IMPULSES IN THE REALITY OF THE THERAPEUTIC RELATIONSHIP

Dr. X, a mental health professional, worked conscientiously in his treatment and the middle phase contained much successful joint work. After a particularly insightful session, I was aware that the advance might arouse some conflict in Dr. X. The next day, he seemed unable to make eye contact. With a mixture of remorse and terror, he told me that, after the previous session, he had felt pleased with himself and proud of our work together.

Then Dr. X didn't know what had happened. As he had listened to his next patient, he found himself distracted, having sexual fantasies and thoughts of having sex with her. He was frightened that he would lose control and even thought of masturbating during the session. He had felt utterly strange, dissociated, then filled with remorse and fear. He felt that I would, even should, report him and have him disqualified. He then wanted to kill all feelings in himself. He felt wicked, an uncontrolled pervert. Dr. X insisted that the treatment seemed to be making him worse and maybe he should stop.

Dr. X continued in this vein for a while. His reversion to closed-system functioning and omnipotent denial of the difference between thoughts and actions was extreme and alarmed me. It took great effort for me to remember that there was another side to him, a competent and sensitive professional who cared for his patients and colleagues. When he talked about his day, I pointed out to him the times he moved quickly past moments of good feeling or accomplishments and raised the question of what function his constant self-denigration could be serving. I had to remind us both that his extreme reaction followed a particularly constructive session when we had worked well together.

He then remembered being asked to rub his mother's naked back when he was a schoolchild. He used to feel giddy, strange and overwhelmed by excitement. As an adolescent he had masturbated with fantasies of losing control and ejaculating all over a woman. It seemed that his helpless rage at his mother for sexually overwhelming and using him had overtaken his loving feelings; his omnipotent reaction was a retaliatory fantasy of attacking his mother with his uncontrolled sexuality. As we talked about his helplessness and rage at the abusive parent, Dr. X returned to describe those sessions of mutually respectful pleasure and love as occurring within and because of the safety of the reality rules and boundaries that were always kept in his treatment with me. He felt that it was a new experience to be treated as a separate, autonomous individual, appreciated for his good qualities and not because of his omnipotent manipulation.

But it made a sharp and painful contrast to his experience with his mother and his previous therapist, and this enraged him. Then he wanted to return to where boundaries, rules and reality limits did not apply, to a closed-system universe where he could go back in time and get revenge. Dr. X talked about the good sessions as "mutative play," but he felt that in his rage he didn't want to play anymore. Like a child who tips over the chessboard when he is losing, he wanted to break the rules, violate the boundaries, deny the reality constraints. Staying with me in the world of reality-attuned pleasures and limitations would mean finally putting aside his omnipotent belief that he could eventually force his mother to love him as the child he really was then. Dr. X was experiencing acutely the conflict between two systems of self-regulation.

COUNTER-REACTIONS AS IMPORTANT SIGNALS

In the third year of his analysis, Mr. G came to the last session of the month, the day before my vacation. I waited a few minutes before noting that Mr. G had not given me the check, as was our custom. Mr. G said that he had forgotten that it was the last session of the month and then said, in a flat tone, "I guess I must be angry with you for taking a vacation." He went on to recount details of his current life events. I remarked on Mr. G's sliding past the question of the check, and he dutifully ran through all the transference wishes we had previously uncovered, especially those of wanting to deny and destroy his envied father.

Mr. G's tone of resignation and my own feelings, ranging from helplessness to a wish to argue, alerted me to the possibility that Mr. G had externalized his conflict on to the treatment relationship. His memory lapse, the effort to provoke a sadomasochistic battle, and his invoking memories of his father all defended against Mr. G's experience of helplessness at being unable to control being left by his analyst/wife/mother. My vacation challenged Mr. G's omnipotent conviction of complete control. He reconstituted his omnipotent beliefs by turning the tables and making beloved people be the ones rejected, abandoned, forced to feel helpless or overwhelmed. He imagined us marooned on a desert island, with me desperately clinging to him for survival, safety and love.

With these defenses still operating on Mr. G's return after my vacation, I became aware of my own moments of sudden sleepiness, a sharp drop in awareness. I tracked those occurrences and found they came in conjunction with material related to separation. It's useful to follow closely not only the patient's ego functions, but also our own, especially those that come into play in working together. I realized that my feeling was one of being dropped, suddenly feeling all alone. So at those times I began to make remarks such as, "I feel you're not here today." Mr. G responded in a definite way, "Yes. Now that you mention it, I notice that I'm talking to you, but I'm somewhere else."

This was the inception of a long, painful, halting period of work that led eventually to re-experiencing and reconstruction of his mother's reactions to any success on his part. Mr. G's mother focused her attention on him only when she worried that he was crippled; an able child did not need her and she dropped him instantly. Mr. G's defensive omnipotent belief that being crippled would ensure attachment, control, safety, special powers, and sexual excitement gradually emerged. His withdrawal in the sessions, first picked up in my feelings of being dropped, presaged a battle inside him over taking the risk to rely on open-system responses to emotional and relationship challenges. My attentiveness to my own reactions was technically central.

MOVING FROM THE MIDDLE PHASE TO PRETERMINATION
Often it is in our own feelings that we first experience intimations of issues around the transition from middle to pretermination phases. The end of the middle phase is marked by a general in-

crease in working through and collaboration, but these are not without conflict. At this point in treatment we often find patients able and willing to work but not to get better. For instance, Mrs. T and I became increasingly skilled at spotting reversions to externalizing transferences, power plays and sadomasochistic patterns of relating, and the intermittent operation of omnipotent, hostile beliefs in control and perfection. Mrs. T was taking on increasing responsibility for self-reflection and observation of the analytic process and she was experiencing more pleasure in all areas. This led me to notice my own occasional thoughts that we might be moving toward pretermination. But Mrs. T made no reference to ending or even thinking about termination.

I found myself musing, occasionally sleepy, and vaguely impatient. Mrs. T began to talk about the financial burden of the treatment and suggested that there was "really nothing more going on here." She thought it was time to just stop. I was taken aback by her proposed manner of ending. My knowledge of all the important work of the termination phase helped me see that Mrs. T was seeking a premature ending.

I talked with Mrs. T about the factors that go into deciding to begin a finishing time. One important element is the patient's feelings about the relationship with the analyst – if Mrs. T had already withdrawn emotionally, it was as if there were no one left to say goodbye to. Mrs. T said angrily, "I've never been left by anyone before, so I'll make sure this is not the first time!" This allowed me to interpret Mrs. T's avoidance of sadness by preemptive control. She felt anxiety and the threat of helplessness in the face of loss of an experience and a person that were really important to her. She was afraid of having real feelings that were not as predictable as her closed-system unhappiness or numbness could be. Those she could control, just as she had tried to control others, including me, by provoking ill treatment in relationships.

Mrs. T and I regained joint work and mutuality in characterizing her conflict between love and power, in effect, between open and closed systems. Looking for and articulating her real, open-system feelings about me and our work together allowed us to see a persisting omnipotent wish to empty the analysis of dynamic activity in order to provoke me to kick her out. She could then be angry with me and avoid feeling helpless in the face of her sadness. She could reinstate her old, closed-system ways to regulate her life.

19

Pretermination

A pretermination phase emerges from a growing sense in both analyst and patient that progressive development has been restored, that there has been a change in the balance between open- and closed-system functioning. Movement and sustained momentum make ending a real possibility. Long ago we noted that the sense of an impetus toward termination was unrelated to abstract goals, but instead relied more on intuition, a feeling of movement in the direction of restoration to the path of progressive development.[91]

The length of the pretermination phase varies, because each patient is different and has a different relationship to issues of successful independent achievement, loss and separation. This is the time when patient and analyst can assess together what remains to be done before termination work can be started. We suggest that the tasks of the pretermination phase to be considered include:

- Maintaining progressive momentum,
- Taking increasing responsibility for joint work,

- Translating insights into action,
- Consolidating open-system, realistic functioning and bringing the possibility of choice between closed and open systems of self-regulation into the foreground,
- Addressing remaining wishes, beliefs, and secrets that protect closed-system, omnipotent functioning,
- Anticipating the work of the termination phase for integration, consolidation, and mourning,
- Assessing tolerance for uncertainty, confidence and readiness for undertaking the tasks of termination.

Each of these tasks evokes conflicts and specific resistances to proceeding with the work, as they each clash directly with beliefs operating in a closed, omnipotent system of defense and self-regulation. Maintaining progressive development and emotional muscle implies change over time, which challenges omnipotent denial of change, growth, generational differences and mortality. Taking increasing mutual responsibility for the joint work runs counter to the omnipotent belief that a relationship of dominance and submission is the only safe and effective way of functioning. Translating insights into action challenges the omnipotent belief that there is no difference between thoughts and action, between fantasy and reality.

With consideration of the possibility of ending we depart from the relative timelessness of the middle phase and actively import the reality dimensions of time and change into the treatment situation, as these are intrinsic to the patient's awareness of open-system goals. This allows a transformed formulation of the current problem as an internal conflict between the patient's open-system wish to change and the closed-system forces that make him reluctant. Each side of this way of conceptualizing the conflict between open- and closed-system functioning can then be examined and worked on. But since no date has been chosen as yet, both patient and analyst have the protected time and space needed to work on conflicts, anxieties, feelings, beliefs and strengths in relation to ending. Much of the work of the pretermination phase involves repeated surveys of closed- and open-system alternatives and the patient's conflicts over choice of responses to feelings of helplessness in the face of stresses from within and without.

Our clinical experience demonstrates that patterns of leave-taking in late adolescence turn out to be important prognosticators of termination issues in treatment. Adult patients often revisit the developmental tasks of late adolescence during the pretermination phase. Setting aside omnipotent beliefs, forming and integrating realistic perceptions of self and other, forging a new relationship between the pleasure and reality principles, thinking about choices of partner, career and life path are all addressed anew in pretermination phase work. These are powerful parallels with the choices between two systems of self-regulation so important in the transition from adolescence to adulthood. Pretermination offers adult patients an opportunity to revisit and rework these adolescent developmental choices and restore developmental momentum.

In the work of the treatment the pretermination phase brings together themes from past phases of the treatment and a reworking of aspects of the patient's history, as well as integration of deeper levels and the inclusion of hitherto undisclosed or undiscussed material. We have also found that our consideration of the nature of the pretermination phase in general pulls together many lines of our theoretical and technical thinking, allowing us to see new connections and integration. In this book we are highlighting our two-systems model and its applications, but in this chapter, we touch on the links to other findings and ideas.

Many years ago we wrote about the disturbance in the pleasure economy that can create a bond between pain and attachment to the mother.[92] The mother of infancy becomes associated with pain; throughout life pain means the presence of the life-giving mother. This is the core of the closed, omnipotent system of self-regulation, further elaborated at each level of development. It reappears with its original attachment aim in the pretermination transference, when a real separation is in the offing. A major cause of stalemate, interminability, or unsatisfactory endings is the operation of sadomasochistic, closed-system modes of self-regulation.

Patients working predominantly with closed-system solutions resist experiences of love and pleasure, particularly in the treatment relationship, because of the terrifying threat of loss and abandonment they connect with good feelings. The work of the middle phases of their treatments allows for sometimes dramatic changes in external functioning in relation to pleasure and satisfaction from competence and effectance. But the attachment to pain can remain in the relationship to the analyst. Here we see the persistence of a closed-system cycle of victimization, pain, justified anger and resentment, overwhelming guilt, and then further victimization.

The closed system offers an illusion of progression. It is, however, a cyclical movement, with lots of noise and activity going nowhere. Ronald Britton wrote about a pathological repetitious cycle "that conceals its static nature. In order for such analysis to be satisfactorily terminated, the cycle needs to become linear, the path of the analysis to be into the unknown future and not a regression into a familiar cyclical sequence."[93]

Neuroscientists describe "functional dystonias," where frequent physical associations create an indissoluble bond between originally independent muscles, like the index and middle fingers of classical guitarists. One finger cannot move without the other; love walks with pain. Related findings describe "brain traps" where two distinct locations in the brain fire simultaneously, like pain and attachment centers, creating a linked experience.[94] Researchers also talk about an "addiction to pain," created when endogenous opioids are released following repeated painful experiences.[95]

These research findings complement the clinical experience of how persistent and intractable the closed system can be. Our efforts to understand the development and functioning of the closed system reflect clinical difficulties in promoting change.

Patients cannot be expected to even consider setting aside their old ways of functioning, ways that have become built-in to their personalities and brains, unless and until they have an alternative possibility. Hence the model of closed and open systems of self-regulation, which offers a way to generate conflict between alternative possible responses to the challenges of life.[96]

The conflict between the open system of love and pleasure in reality relationships and achievements and the closed-system cycles of safety and power in pain and suffering is worked on throughout treatment. During pretermination the challenge is to grapple with the patient's continuing conflicts over open-system developmental momentum, expressed in a pull to ruin real pleasures, maintain painful attachments, deny love and resist change. The work of pretermination is to consolidate open-system functioning and analyze these remaining obstacles.

In the closed system there is an omnipotent denial of time and change. But the new presence of the reality of time in the pretermination phase confronts that denial and brings this conflict within the ego into the foreground. Anticipating the possibility of an actual ending and engaging in the tasks of the pretermination phase stretches the patient's emotional capacities. Grappling with the ineluctable reality of time provides an opportunity to strengthen ego functions and build emotional muscle to combat the pull back into closed-system functioning and promote open-system living. A cycle of positive feelings is being created, where success leads to feelings of effectiveness and competence, which lead in turn to pleasure, which strengthens the motivation for mastery and progressive development.

The role of love is fundamental to our understanding of development and functioning. We have written elsewhere about varieties of love, the perverse sadomasochistic feelings and power dynamics of the closed system, and the reality-based, generative and creative love of the open system of self-regulation.[97] Much of our thinking is based on Freud's last revision of his concept of Eros, a basic instinct whose aim is to bind together, establish greater unities, and to preserve them. Thus Eros comprises love, sex, attachment, affection, affiliation, generativity, creativity – all the domains of feeling, thinking, action and being that relate to life and growth. Eros can then be seen as an overarching definer of open-system functioning, in which pleasure, self-regulation and self-esteem are based on competent, respectful, creative interactions with reality.

Only in the context of love and respect for the patient as a separate person can the therapist hand over initiative and responsibility. Awareness of the distinction between the two systems of self-regulation allows the therapist to feel objective love, love of the real skills of self and other used separately and together, love of the work accomplished, and love for the unique, capable person the patient has become. Only with security in objective love can the therapist experience and use moments of hatred for the patient's desperate attempts to fall back on omnipotent manipulation to destroy the therapeutic achievement and the competent skills of both partners.

In relation to pretermination, we want to emphasize the important relationship between love and sadness. People are only sad to lose someone they love; we don't miss people unless we love them. But those can be painful emotions and many are afraid of them. Since both love and sadness are central to the experience of termination, pretermination invokes anticipation of those feelings. Both patients and analysts may respond with open-system mastery or with reversion to closed-system pathological defenses.

PATIENT TASKS: PUTTING INSIGHTS INTO ACTION, INTERNALIZATION OF MASTERY OF ALLIANCE TASKS, INDEPENDENT THERAPEUTIC WORK, MAINTAIN PROGRESSIVE MOMENTUM

The move from the end of the middle phase to the pretermination phase requires focus on the task of translating insights into action, as the patient may be very willing to work on issues by talking about them in treatment, but not to get better.[98] The analyst may only gradually realize that the good work in the treatment is not having an impact on the patient's daily life. The first technical step to helping the patient accomplish this task is to point out the disparity and wonder with the patient about his not remarking it and on what it may represent. This apparently simple question leads to a restatement of the goals of the treatment.

The idea of a pretermination phase can help protect a treatment against premature termination. It can also have an important effect on situations of stalemate or interminability. In the course of treatment important, legitimate ego needs have been recognized and met through the therapeutic relationship. The needs to be felt with, listened to, understood, validated and admired for progressive achievements are basic to everyone. All partners in a treatment should address the question of who will fulfill these needs for the patient when the therapy ends. Can the child elicit an appropriate response from important people in his life? Can the adult patient find people who will be empathic, loving and willing to share his feelings and thoughts? These basic human needs can be met by parents, friends, mentors, husbands and wives. A final resistance to ending analysis may appear in a reluctance to put the insights of treatment into action by seeking appropriate people or eliciting needed responses from available people. If the analyst remains the only person the patient can really talk to, a major area of resistance, probably in both people, is affecting progressive movement and must be addressed.

Practicing working more autonomously and responsibly in the treatment, in the presence of a therapist who clearly enjoys and engages with a patient's increasing open-system mastery of the alliance tasks, allows a patient to internalize the skills in the ego. A therapeutic relationship with an increasing proportion of realistic open-system mutual regard is the setting for expansion of ego capacities and consolidation of open-system choices.

But even the idea of ending can be daunting and usually arouses old fears and conflicts. Fluctuations in the nature of the transference, interferences with connection with the analyst, and reworking of past themes and issues are the norm during the pretermination phase.

THERAPIST TASK: ALLOW FOR PATIENT'S INDEPENDENT THERAPEUTIC WORK

To work effectively with the strong feelings and intense conflicts that arise at this time, we as therapists must feel sincerely comfortable with our own pretermination alliance tasks – to relinquish initiative without withdrawal, to allow for and acknowledge the patient's increasingly effective autonomous functioning without being over-whelmed by feelings of abandonment, loss, envy or defeat. We have to be able to let go of the extremely gratifying and satisfying experi-ence of active, competent use of our own egos and still feel that we are important and useful to the patient. We have to be able to tolerate the reality of uncertainty, not knowing what the final outcome will be and what the future will hold for the patient. This is a juncture at which we become newly aware of the importance of a wide range of sources of emotional supplies and self-esteem for ourselves, since dependence on a patient's neediness will cripple both therapeutic partners and bring the treatment to a standstill, expressed in an artificial termination, a prolonged unproductive therapy, or a post-termination boundary violation.

Erna Furman has drawn on her observations of mothers and toddlers to describe a sequence of engagement that can usefully be applied to therapeutic work with patients of all ages.[99] At first the parent *does for* the child, then *does with* the child, and finally *stands by to admire* as the child *does it for herself*. This simple sequence carries profound implications, for it is the root of objec-tive love, based on realistic open-system respect for the other as a separate person. We begin in treatment by doing a lot of the work, showing the patient how the method will work. Then we work to-gether through the middle phase. Eventually, in the pretermination phase, we can stand by to admire as the patient takes on increasing autonomy in the joint endeavor. By termination the patient is ready to work independently.

Many causes of premature termination are dealt with in the middle phase. However, once the real possibility of ending has been raised, the conflict between the two systems can become much more acute, leading to flareups of old ways of dealing with anxiety. This is a danger point for the treatment, as there may be a reversion to closed-system equating of autonomy with separation and loss. The patient may attempt to avoid the pain of loss by shifting back from a differentiated relationship to an externalizing transference. The part of the patient that feels like a lonely, abandoned child may be externalized on to the therapist, who can then be left behind by the powerful patient as parent in the transference. The first sign of such a shift can be detected in the quality of working together, as the patient may become subtly sarcastic, impatient, or patronizingly tolerant. As one patient said, "Since I can do the work without you, you're useless and I don't need you any more." Independent work has become perverted, made into a hostile method of control and discarding of the other. This stance can easily provoke the therapist into hurt retaliation, as the patient appears to be devaluing and destroying the work of years.

The analyst's hurt feeling is the clue to the left-behind externalization, and the urge to retaliate alerts the therapist to the hostility included in the patient's stance. There are likely to be repetitions of this interaction as patient and therapist work through profound, primitive fears of abandonment, sadistic impulses to dominate or submit, competitive and comparative concerns, shame and guilt, anxiety over differences and disagreements, and so forth, all motives that have led in the past to closed-system efforts at solution.

SIGNIFICANT OTHER/PARENT TASK: ENJOY AND VALIDATE PROGRESSION

Parents and significant others have the task of enjoying and validating the patient's progression. Central to work with parents during this phase is helping them shift from the mode of doing emotional work for the child to the important stance of being there to validate, admire, and promote progressive moves. Formulating their task in these terms allows for assessment of parental readiness to undertake the work needed to accomplish termination. Adult patients may need focused attention on the importance of bringing their partner into synchrony with their progress. Remaining marital conflicts sometimes surface at this point in the treatment and must be addressed before the patient can move on.

CLINICAL EXAMPLES OF
TWO-SYSTEMS TECHNIQUE

CLOSED-SYSTEM SEQUESTERING OF
OPEN-SYSTEM INTERACTIONS IN THE TREATMENT

Dr. E was a middle-aged professional man who had previously completed a 5-year analysis with a senior analyst. A few years after the end of that treatment he called his analyst for further help as he had suffered a return of overwhelming panic and inability to sleep that caused massive interference in his work, which required very fine hand-eye coordination. His analyst had retired and the patient was referred to me.

Referrals or calls from people about a second or third treatment come for a variety of reasons. Often it is possible to spot some omission or serious collusion during the termination phase that then ruined an otherwise good enough earlier therapy. Brief work in relation to avoidance of some termination issues is frequently sufficient to restore the person to the path of progressive development. In the case of Dr. E, most of these had actually been canvassed in his earlier treatment and going over them again made no difference to his anxiety.

What did reduce the intensity of his panic was settling into a return to analysis, where many of his basic needs were once more being met. Interpretation had little effect, but, as he said, "It's such a relief to have someone listen, take me seriously and have some sympathy and concern for me. It's very lonely and cold out there." Dr. E had ended a good analysis and a good termination a much changed person, except for the fact that he remained locked in a cold, unempathic marriage with a very disturbed woman who armored herself with unresponsiveness, excessive drinking and a state of psychic numbness. She acted as if Dr. E didn't exist except as someone who took out the garbage. The previous work had recognized the frustrations of this marriage, and Dr. E's decision to stay in the marriage was considered an accommodation for the sake of the children.

What had gone unrecognized was the degree to which the open-system interaction between Dr. E and his analyst had given him an experience of mutuality, respect, and human interchange that he relied on. He had not generated any other resources for meeting these legitimate basic needs. It was almost impossible to function with his disturbed wife as his only human contact.

After a time of work together Dr. E again reached the point where he was functioning well, without undue anxiety. His treatment stalled. I commented on how everything seemed to be going well, and I wondered why he wasn't mentioning finishing. He said he was wondering this too. This is a choice point for the analyst. If we go by external criteria, why shouldn't he stop? I could have said, "Well, since we both agree that significant changes have taken place, why don't we pick a date?" But this is what had happened in his previous treatment. I said to him that we were in a time of thinking through readiness to say goodbye and there were numerous aspects to consider.

The most important one emerged almost immediately. Dr. E said, "You're the only one I can meaningfully talk to, so why should I finish?" The goal for the pretermination phase could then be defined to include understanding what had kept him isolated and tied to his wife, and what interfered now with his seeking new, sustaining relationships. As Dr. E wryly put it, "How're you gonna keep 'em down on the farm, after they've seen Paree?"

This pretermination period was long, as many earlier determinants emerged and had to be worked through. Eventually, he moved out of the house, met other women and began a long-term relationship with a warm and accepting person. Only at this point could we revisit his readiness to finish and move forward to picking a date and starting the intense work of the termination phase.

The idea of the pretermination phase helped in this case to resolve the stalemate, and also prevented a forced termination from the side of the impatient analyst. Additional crucial work on more underlying conflicts between two systems of self-regulation was needed before Dr. E could move forward. Working together to address Dr. E's conflicts over putting insights into action and taking realistic responsibility for momentum in his relationships inside and out of treatment revitalized the analysis and led to a mutually enhancing ending.

MOTIVES FOR RESISTANCE TO CHANGE

A middle-aged man in treatment for some years seemed to get great enjoyment out of the emotional and intellectual interchange, but the insights achieved did not affect his external life. Mr. H still felt deeply insecure and unfulfilled in professional and personal relations. He had suffered rather extreme childhood situations of abandonment and loss. As it became more evident that insights were not being put into action, his belief in his own omnipotence emerged clearly. He should not have to do anything to get what he wanted. External pain and dysfunction were the route to keeping the analyst/mother from leaving. He said, "If my outside world improves, then what is there for us to do together. If I don't need you, you'll drop me and I'll never see you again, and I can't sustain another loss. It is clear that being with you is more important than pleasure in my life."

Being so valued and needed offers a powerful temptation to therapists to retain the patient as a source of gratification. Theoretical models that don't include open-system goals for ending treatment and/or minimize the importance of a termination process may rationalize interminable treatments.[100] For some months further Mr. H and I worked again on his equation of separation and death. This time we were able to discern and address the aggressive component of his fear of losing me. It appeared in terms of how his catastrophic vision of the future without even an internal image of me represented his killing me off in his mind. Once we were able to work through his efforts to protect me from his omnipotently murderous criticisms and disappointments, we were able to look together at the high price he paid to retain his closed-system functioning by staying in treatment and not getting on with his life.

RISK OF PREMATURE TERMINATION BY CLOSED-SYSTEM REPETITIONS

Mrs. M, a talented artist, had made use of her long treatment to regain her creative functioning and vastly improve her relationships with her family and friends. All positive signs for moving toward ending were there. But, one day, she announced that she would be ending right away. She was coming in prepared for a fight, sure that I would oppose her wish to finish. I agreed that there had been substantive changes and said, "It is important to be sure that we are both ready to do the hard work of saying goodbye. This is a pre-goodbye time that we can use to strengthen the emotional muscles needed for the task of ending." Mrs. M was surprised at my response and relaxed. I said that, in this getting ready time, we would want to explore whether there were areas that we had not looked at.

I then wondered why there was little mention of her husband's thoughts and reactions to the changes she had made. Mrs. M was reluctant to talk about this, and avoided the issue for some weeks. Eventually she said she was sure I had noticed her difficulty in admitting that the idea of ending really came from him. "He's eager for me to stop," she said. "He puts it in terms of money, but that's just a cover-up of his real motive. He wants us to resume the kinky sex we used to have. He thinks that I'll change back once I'm not in treatment. He says that, with my therapist out of the picture, there will be nothing to stop us." As Mrs. M talked more about how hard it was to address this, she was able to say that she had hated those sexual practices, but feared that she didn't have the moral courage to stand up to her husband about them. This made it clear to both of us that more work was needed before we could pick a date and enter into a termination phase.

The work with Mrs. M focused for a time on the distinction between secrecy and privacy.[101] She had long lived a double life, keeping secrets from her parents and then her husband, and brought this pattern into her analysis, where we worked on it throughout. Now, in the context of thinking about termination, she had once again created secrets that were vehicles for closed-system power dynamics in the treatment relationship, as well as outside.

This vignette also highlights another common effort of the pretermination phase, that is, the exploration of remaining secrets or withheld experiences. By turning her private inner life into a secret, she could continue living in a closed system where her pain justified omnipotent actions, like having affairs. In this pretermination phase she began to see that her private feelings could be the main resource for a realistic, open, loving relationship with herself and significant other people, including her analyst and husband.

Mrs. M began sharing her self more with her husband, finding pleasure in feeling close to him as she had not done for years. He then began to appreciate the contrast between the excitement of perverse sexuality and the deep pleasure of intimacy. Continued work on the distinction between secrecy and privacy and her use of secrets to protect her private world allowed Mrs. M to talk about her own true wishes to end, but her fear of losing my love if she asserted herself. We could then see her closed-system secrets as an omnipotent defense against feeling helpless and alone. Her true self was in her private world, which she had felt too weak to protect. Extended work on the pretermination task of valuing, enjoying and realizing the realistic power that resided in her freedom to choose to share her private self, in contrast to the illusory power of sadomasochistic secrets, led eventually to genuine progressive movement and an authentic decision to begin and achieve a good goodbye.

For Mrs. M, the pretermination phase prevented a premature flight from treatment, which would have recapitulated or re-enacted in the transference her pathological closed-system adolescent patterns of dealing with her important relationships by running away. For the analyst, the idea of the necessity for pretermination work allowed for a non-defensive, therapeutic response. Pretermination offered an open-system alternative to a fruitless, sadomasochistic confrontation with her defenses. The idea of pretermination allows both people to go together into a shared ego arena to examine readiness and the state of the treatment.

THE PERSISTENCE OF OMNIPOTENT BELIEFS

Dr. W was a prominent young academic, a star with a prodigious output of important papers and books in his field. External signs of success accelerated, including tenure at a young age and attractive offers from other universities. Each of Dr. W's brilliant papers or books was, however, done at a feverish pitch as if his life depended on completion. After publication he bound each paper, and added it to the books on a special shelf set aside for his productions. He then typically went into a depression that lasted until he started the next writing project. Then he would again immerse himself in total preoccupation with research and writing.

He had come to therapy after being given elsewhere an initial diagnosis of bi-polar illness. I agreed with his wish to see what he could do with psychoanalysis before "going down the medication route." By the fourth year of treatment, there had been significant internal and external changes. For the first time, he allowed himself to have some life outside his work, to enjoy relationships with men and women, and to have a pleasurable relationship with a woman he planned to marry. His teaching had shifted from feeling like an enormous interference and burden to a source of pleasure. He enjoyed giving lectures, running seminars, and being a mentor to doctoral students who enrolled especially to work with him.

In treatment, after the first years of painful and difficult work, he began to find it fascinating and rewarding, and he could see its immediate effects on his moods, his work, and his relationships. He mentioned the possibility of ending his therapy and I agreed that all signs seemed to point that way. What remained to be done before we started a termination phase? Together we looked at what had changed and what hadn't. We agreed that, with most other areas going well, we could focus in a pretermination phase on his continued lack of pleasure in his writing. He no longer plunged into depression on publishing, but, other than relief, he experienced no joy or pride.

In fact he always emphasized the incompleteness or deficiencies in his work rather than the innovative ideas recognized by his colleagues. We had worked throughout his treatment on the many meanings of this closed-system stance. We had made solid inroads on his co-opting of his extraordinary cognitive skills and talents to the service of maintaining defensive omnipotent beliefs since childhood. He had always experienced his intellectual productions as responses to external demands, never as real open-system pleasures in themselves that he could own. He felt that being smart was what made him stand out in his family; it was the only way he could compete with his beautiful, talented sister and his handsome, athletic older brother. As part of an important piece of middle phase work he arrived at and integrated his rage at his experience of parents who did not love him unconditionally, but only if he were smart.

As we explored his lack of pleasure in the context of work remaining to do he produced a series of associations that led to his hidden belief that, if he could discover my expectations for him in the treatment, then he could fulfill my wish and win my love. If I wanted him to understand this last piece of the puzzle, he would do so, and then he would get what he needs from me. With a clear developmental image in mind, I said that he sounded to me like a child who feels helpless to get what he needs and then thinks that he has figured out a way. Dr. W was actually helpless in childhood to change his mother from a depressed and incompetent parent to someone responsive to his actions and dependably available. He tried to use his intelligence to feel effective in relation to his mother. Whether it's a child doing well in school or acting up, using naughty behavior to get negative attention, the point is the legitimate deep human need to feel effective. It may or may not actually work, but what matters is that the child has found something that makes him *think* he is no longer helpless. This can become a lifelong closed-system belief in power to make someone else respond the way the individual needs.

We had worked on the idea that being smart got him special attention from his mother, but now, in the context of pretermination, we could consider that what it may actually have done was to give him the illusion (perhaps necessary at the time) that he wasn't helpless. This had allowed him to generate and hold on to the belief that he had the power to force the love he needed. He could deny the reality that each person is only in charge of his or her own feelings.

Dr. W was startled. He then said that his shelf of publications was nearly filled up. Even though he had reached a point in his professional career when he no longer had to publish, he felt driven by the wish to fill up the shelf. He had a conviction, a hope that something special and magical would happen when he reached that goal. He was silent for a long time, then said, "I think I've had that dream for a long time, for as long as I can remember. Each time I've reached a goal I would feel let down, and then create another goal. What you said about my being smart is hard to integrate. Not hard really, but emotionally hard. I can feel myself fighting the idea, wanting to argue, overwhelm you with my smarts. Can it be true that I've used my mind like a placebo, in order to maintain the illusory belief that my mother loved me *because* I was smart? I feel I can never give up that idea; without it I would sink into despair and never work again."

He became quite depressed over the next few weeks, to a point where I was thinking of a psychiatric consultation. I shared my concern with Dr. W, but added that mostly I felt that we were getting to the core issue of his depression. After each dazzling intellectual success he realized that it made no difference to his mother's capacity to meet his needs. From his descriptions of a fragile, anxious and depressed mother who abused alcohol and medications, we could surmise that her love and attention to him could only have been intermittent, dependent more on her own mental state than on anything he did or didn't do.[102]

Dr. W responded by saying that he had recalled in the last few days that she did in fact notice his achievements, but then used them to attribute to him a precocious independence that made her withdrawal acceptable. He remembered her saying, "Oh, my dear, you're so smart, I'm sure you can take care of yourself while I go upstairs to rest." Dr. W was no longer depressed, but he was sad and angry and then sorry for his mother, who was so ill and unable to enjoy her extraordinary children. He spent time visiting each of his siblings, something he had avoided for years, and they shared the pain of growing up with an absent father and a sick mother.

I asked him how he thought these feelings applied to the work he had accomplished in analysis. Dr. W began to talk about his joy in the process, the excitement of discovery, and the pleasure of feeling his mind working effectively without extraneous demands like the idea that success in therapeutic work would make me love him.

Not long after, he began a new project and described his pleasure at "wrapping [his] mind around a new idea," in crafting a sentence that clearly expresses his thought, synthesizing, elaborating, criticizing and then going beyond his previous work. One day he broke into a broad smile and said, "I feel like an adolescent when he discovers the joy of sex. I write not because I have to or that it will achieve some magical goal like the hand of the princess. I write because I love it – I'm good at it, I'm smart and I enjoy that."

Then his smile disappeared. He looked sad and said, "But I still feel I have to fill up that shelf. The old belief is still there." I noted that his old belief has been part of him for a long time and will never disappear. Treatment, however, had opened up the possibility of other, open-system sources of reality-based security and pleasure. "Here in our relationship we can see the tension between these two ways of being – using all your skills and talents to get my attention and approval, or taking your own pleasure in your competence and sharing that with me, so that I can enjoy your pride and good feelings. I can stand by to admire." I said that now I thought he was ready to pick a date for ending. The book shelf, as representing the conflict between the two potential systems of self-regulation, was one of the things we would work on in the context of saying goodbye.

CONFLICTS IN THE TRANSITION FROM PRETERMINATION TO TERMINATION

When it came to picking a date for termination, Mrs. T again reverted to an externalizing, sadomasochistic transference relationship to me.[103] She insisted that I should decide, with a fantasy that I was persecuting her by asking her to make the choice. Then she could be justified in her anger and could fight with me and storm out of treatment. I recalled what we had learned about her wish to control the feelings between us in order to avoid the pain of mourning. I suggested that she was using her sense of victimization to retain an illusion of power over the situation.

Mrs. T brought in a dream of a nuclear holocaust. Associations quickly led to her conviction that her feelings could annihilate us both, that I would be blasted into the void of space after termination unless she retained control by making me a failure. This stemmed from her core omnipotent belief, her delusion that she could keep me alive as an available mother only by locking us both into an angry, sadomasochistic timeless paralysis.

The next session was a breezy, sunny day. Mrs. T came in smiling ruefully and remarked as soon as she settled on the couch that she had noticed the lovely morning. She was remembering the several springs that had passed during her analysis, and realized that she had only recently begun to even notice the smell and the soft air. She had been thinking that we had been through lots of hard times together, but couldn't deny that there had also been some good times. It occurred to her that she had to give me credit for my contribution if she were going to take any credit for hers. This acknowledgment contained her realization that I was a separate, autonomous person whose thoughts and feelings were not under her control. It was also evidence of her recovered capacity to work independently, a milestone alliance achievement of the pretermination phase. She was then able to move forward into starting a termination phase.

20

Termination

THERAPEUTIC TASK: SAYING A GOOD GOODBYE

From the beginnings of psychoanalysis and psychotherapy there have been many examples of good therapies being ruined by misconceived and mishandled terminations. We have written about the concepts of the therapeutic alliance and the two systems as guides through the labyrinth of competing and contradictory technical precepts on termination.[104] In terms of content, we must think through what we really lose at the end of a treatment and what we imagine or fear we are losing. We are helped in this effort by staying mindful of the therapeutic alliance tasks for this phase and distinguishing, as in the earlier phases, between love as part of an open system and the hostile control that masquerades as love but in fact emanates from a closed, omnipotent sadomasochistic system.

Setting aside infantile wishes from all levels of development, including closed-system belief in the omnipotence of the self or of others, seems a frightening and painful loss for both patient and analyst. But the work of the earlier phases has allowed for the establishment of alternative sources of security and self-esteem in realistic open-system achievements and representations. Much of the work of the termination phase is drawing the distinction between the illusory loss of unreal fantasy gains and the real loss of the setting, the analyst, and the special therapeutic relationship.

All being well, at this point the therapeutic alliance is at peak efficiency, open-system solutions are now available, and both people have many more resources to resolve conflicts and work through potentially traumatic events. The termination phase is a time when the analytic achievements can be seen and tested. A wide range of feelings can be experienced, owned, used as signals and guides to further actions. Emotions such as disappointment, disillusionment, and sadness are particularly intense during this time; detailed work on defenses against and working through these emotions allows the patient to mourn and grow from the experience. In particular, the loss of the therapeutic relationship can be mourned and the skills acquired through mastery of the alliance tasks internalized as a capacity for self-analysis and creative living.

A good goodbye to treatment depends on the patient's, the analyst's, and the significant others' capacities to bear feelings, mourn losses and internalize good aspects of the other. Each of the therapeutic alliance tasks for patient, therapist, and parents or significant others is a manifestation or objective description of an aspect of the open system. Such a conceptualization helps us maintain criteria internal to the clinical situation for the assessment of obstacles, change, and eventual termination. Mastery and internalization of the therapeutic alliance tasks propels the patient through the treatment trajectory, to arrive at the termination phase ready to face its tasks and work toward its goals.

Good goodbyes draw on many open-system capacities.

The overall aim of the termination phase is to consolidate open-system functioning, which includes the capacity to be with another and oneself; the capacity to work together with another and alone in the presence of the other in a creative, mutually-enhancing way; the capacity to be autonomous without having to separate and to retain autonomy when separate; the capacity to say goodbye in a mutually-enriching way, acknowledging mourning and so internalizing the positive aspects of the relationship. These all contribute to the self-analytic function.

The possibility of open-system functioning has been a goal of treatment from the start. The extent of open-system functioning has been assessed together during the pretermination phase and will now be tested, strengthened, and consolidated under the stress of a real, immutable ending date.

PATIENT TASKS: MOURNING AND INTERNALIZATION

During the termination phase the therapeutic alliance is strong and effective, but there is also intense resistance and conflict issuing from old closed-system patterns. There are several tasks for patients during the termination phase. They are:

- To consolidate competent, open-system functioning so that there is a genuine conflict between old omnipotent closed-system solutions and newly-acquired or reactivated open-system functioning.
- To work through revived conflicts in the context of saying goodbye
- To set aside infantile closed-system beliefs, especially in omnipotent power to control others and their feelings
- To help others in their lives keep pace with their changes and their feelings
- To mourn the loss of the unique relationship, setting, and ways of working established in the treatment
- To internalize the loving, supportive, and ego-enhancing aspects of the therapeutic relationship.
- To consolidate the capacity to find pleasure in working with others and alone toward creative solutions to life challenges, including self-analysis when needed.

Termination is a time when patients can practice reading their own feelings, monitoring the activity of closed- or open-system emotional functioning. Anger, for instance, generally has an important open-system role as a signal of something a person doesn't like. The signal triggers assessment of the situation to discern the cause of the trouble and do something about it, or to recognize that there is nothing one can do.[105] Experience of this process is satisfying in itself, as the person feels the effective functioning of the mind working harmoniously.

Anger as a state, on the other hand, is a manifestation of the closed system. Overt or covert hostility, unfettered rage, and the effort at revenge are all part of the powerful network of closed-system solutions the person devised during childhood or adolescence to deal with overwhelming, potentially traumatic experience.

Retaining the idea of revenge can be a secret insurance against helplessness that patients may cling to even during the termination phase. Beyond that function, hostile and vengeful fantasies and preoccupations are exciting. There is gratification associated with the discharge of aggression. Research has demonstrated that revenge triggers the same brain centers that desire, drugs and desserts do.[106] We have all experienced the internal surge of power associated with thinking of the most cutting riposte, the just deserts, and the humiliation of a rival. This genuine power of closed-system gratifications – the addictive, sometimes ecstatic rush – has to be acknowledged by patient and therapist, along with the recognition that dependable, reality-based pleasures will never produce the same result. What matters is the choice available for sustained, safe satisfactions, gratifications and pleasures.

Another arena for work is facing that the reality of ending confronts closed-system denial of change, time, and the constraints of reality. Disappointment also belongs in the open system. It comes from an awareness and acceptance of the realistic limitations of self, others, and life. Accessing idealized expectations and fantasies is extremely important in the termination phase, in order to deal with realistic disappointments in the analyst, the analysis, and the self. Then there is disappointment of realistic wishes and goals, which is also crucial to acknowledge. Treatment takes time, and there is a

The reality of ending confronts denial.

timeless element to it, especially in the middle phase. But, in the meantime, actual time is passing, and there are certain real life passages, like childbearing, parenting, career choices and so forth that occupy a certain window of time. If pathology or circumstance has interfered with fulfillment of realistic wishes in those windows, both patient and therapist have to deal with this disappointment together.

All authors agree that mourning is a major aspect of termination, but it has not been made explicit in the literature what or who is being mourned, nor how this relates to sadness, depression, or the ability to choose. Analysts tend to speak about mourning the loss of a person, a phase of life, or a fantasy. In a single-track psychoanalytic theory of development, much is made of how "normal" omnipotence has to be mourned and then relinquished. With a dual-track, two-system model we can posit that a belief is never mourned or gone but rather it is set aside. The omnipotent belief remains a potential response forever, but therapeutic work has helped the patient find open-system alternatives to choose from, perhaps transforming a pathological belief into a wish or fantasy, a delusion into an illusion.

Setting aside organizing convictions may be painful, but the pain may be likened to withdrawal from an addictive substance. It is a process different from mourning, as there is no subsequent internalization and identification. In the closed system separation is equated with loss of control of others and of feelings, and therefore a depressive response in defense against rage and helplessness may be an expected reaction when the patient reverts to attempts at omnipotent control.

The crucial issue is sadness, which is present only when there is love, which means there is a genuine loss. Thus sadness exists in the realm of open-system functioning, with its connection to real experience. We can only mourn the loss of someone we love and, through the mourning, internalize aspects of the person and qualities of the relationship. What is truly mourned by patient and therapist at a good goodbye is the unique working and loving relationship that enhanced each person and will now persist only internally as they separate.[107] What each can internalize and identify with is a greater understanding of the realistic interdependence and independence found in a mutually respectful relationship of autonomous individuals.

The restoration of the capacity to choose and the tools forged in the accomplishment of the open-system therapeutic alliance tasks equip patients for the lifelong struggle against the potential to resolve conflicts with closed-system, sadomasochistic, omnipotent beliefs.

THERAPIST'S TASK: MOURNING AND STEADFASTNESS

Termination challenges therapists too, as we are all vulnerable to the same deep anxieties about time, mortality, loss and change. There are several aspects to the analyst's task:

- To allow the patient's realistic sadness, grief and mourning
- To deal with our own sense of losing an important relationship, a connection to the patient's whole world, and a unique opportunity to exercise our skills
- To analyze to the end and not give in to pressures from within or without to alter the way of working and the nature of the relationship.
- To assess results realistically and come to terms with open-system 'good enough' endings.

Termination evokes intense feelings in therapists. There is often surprising, uncharacteristic behavior; blind spots arise even for experienced clinicians. These may indicate the presence of powerful countertransference conflicts and defenses. For example, there may be a sudden shift to self-disclosure when this was not part of regular technique earlier in the treatment. Therapists may resort to management rather than engage in joint exploration. Sometimes the analyst withdraws preemptively and there ensues a loss of emotional intensity or vitality, with both patient and analyst feeling there is nothing much left to say or do. Assessing results and managing disappointments challenge the therapist's open-system capacities.

The assumption that therapists have only a neutral, professional reaction to termination is an omnipotent belief disproven by honest self-examination, open exchange with trusted colleagues, a cursory acquaintance with the radical departures from their own standard clinical techniques during termination, and a reading of the literature on analysts' fantasies at termination.[108] Proper technique and experience help, but nothing can completely protect a therapist from the pain of separation and loss. With each patient, we have been privileged to know a full world of people, complex networks of relationships past and present, the characteristics of another line of work, the development of children, life passages in families, and so forth. When patients leave, in a sense, whole worlds leave with them.

SIGNIFICANT OTHERS/PARENT TASK: SUPPORT AND VALIDATION

Partners and parents have had a significant relationship with the therapist, directly or indirectly. It takes confidence and patience to support a spouse or a child or adolescent through a deep experience, while respecting their separateness and their privacy. The others in the patient's life may have feelings and reactions of their own that have to be taken into account.

CLINICAL EXAMPLES OF
TWO-SYSTEMS TECHNIQUES

In the introduction to the treatment and technique section of this book, we noted the dimensions that a two-systems model highlights. They are 'what we attend to,' the 'actual interventions we do or don't make,' and 'what this model allows us to include' as what is specifically and legitimately psychoanalytic. Termination gathers the themes from all phases of treatment. At the same time, many analysts depart radically from their usual technical stance at this point in treatment, and may rationalize what they do. We find that a two-systems model helps us stay anchored under the pressures of termination. A two-systems model allows for inclusion of a broad spectrum of techniques, while simultaneously protecting a psychoanalytic frame and range of interventions.

PRESSURE TO ALTER THE RELATIONSHIP

Mrs. F

I was pleased and enthusiastic about the beginning of the termination phase in Mrs. F's treatment. She talked one day about how her family was making the choices about her child's entry to high school. I was surprised to find myself on the verge of telling her where my children had attended and how we had weighed the different factors, since such self-disclosure had not been part of the treatment before. There was some internal pressure to rationalize the impulse on the grounds that the relationship had reached a more realistic basis. Thinking about this after the session, however, I realized that I was going to miss hearing about Mrs. F's children, whose development I had followed for some time. I was saying goodbye not only to this patient but also to her whole network of relationships, which had become part of my mental landscape.

Two-systems thinking helped me recognize the pull to a closed-system interaction, where I would be imposing my experience on her, using her to meet my needs to hold on to the connection to her world, and denying the reality of the sadness involved in bidding farewell to her and her whole family.

Mr. R

As Mr. R moved into the termination phase and simultaneously moved forward in many areas of his life, he spoke about whether he should buy a new house. Over several sessions, I realized that I had formed strong opinions about his choice and wanted to tell him what to do. On reflection, it became clear that Mr. R was successfully pulling us both back into a closed-system interaction. The tug within me related to no longer feeling so important and necessary to his life decisions as we neared the end. I could then take up with him the ongoing conflict inside him between trusting his now reliable realistic open-system capacities to make judgments and the old sadomasochistic wishes to submit to an authority figure, which reminded us both of the changes he had made in his treatment.

Mr. E

In the middle of the termination phase Mr. E took a preplanned short vacation break. On his return, he described at length his plans for the future. I found myself drifting off, daydreaming about my own upcoming vacation. This was a reactive tit-for-tat withdrawal with both of us avoiding the immediate experience of saying goodbye in the present. Open-system focus includes the time dimension and raises our consciousness to the myriad, often subtle, manipulations that we can make around temporal dimensions.

Mrs. S

Mrs. S, who had been abandoned in early childhood by her father, was reunited with him in adolescence only to be sexually abused by him. As we approached the end of a long, fruitful treatment she began talking about her researches on abuse. She knew that her scientific interest was one way of dealing with her experience with her father. Then she described extending the research to boundary violations between therapists and patients. She noted how frequently this occurred and said that professional associations accept the legitimacy of sexual relationships a year or two after the end of treatment. Mrs. S quickly realized that she must be talking about us, and this enabled us to revisit her adolescent effort to deal with abandonment and loss by submitting to a sadomasochistic sexual interaction.

Without taking blame on herself, Mrs. S could encompass the reality that she had felt powerful through her sexuality to attract and keep her father in a way she was powerless to do as a little child. Her capacity to know this about herself came directly from work throughout the treatment on closed-system thinking and behavior as a solution to a threatening situation and on the simultaneous existence of both closed- and open-system dimensions of experience. This work continued at termination, where now I could remind her of the hostility intrinsic to the sadomasochistic relationship; Mrs. S agreed and added that she still could only think about all of this at the same time because she knew that I understood, but wouldn't act on her seductive efforts. This allowed us to acknowledge her reluctance to set aside the omnipotent conviction of irresistibility, acknowledge the reality of her attractiveness, and live with the painful, but not devastating, sadness of saying an open-system goodbye that was not an abandonment.

PERSISTENCE OF CLOSED-SYSTEM OMNIPOTENT BELIEFS

Mr. Q

When Mr. Q came for treatment because he was unable to concentrate on his work, he described the unremittingly cruel and sadistic teasing he suffered at the hands of his siblings throughout his childhood. This material came up repeatedly throughout his treatment, particularly as he worked through his disappointment with his mother, who was too depressed to intervene.

These memories habitually triggered intense rage and thoughts of revenge. His exceptional intelligence and imagination had been coopted to serve these preoccupations, which led to his extreme inhibition in functioning. For a long time, however, Mr. Q was not interested in getting rid of his rageful preoccupation, but only in ridding himself of the inhibitions. The work of the treatment revealed the underlying omnipotent belief that he could somehow go back in time and visit revenge on them and undo what had happened and its impact.

By the end of the treatment, Mr. Q was very successful in his creative and demanding work, had married and had children, and felt much more comfortable with his strengths. He commented that he seldom had his old revenge daydreams. He accepted that he had better ways to protect himself; besides, his brothers were now very different and they got along very well. But, he said, "I do miss the charge, the jolt of adrenalin when I think of ways to destroy them. I know it sounds crazy, but I'm reluctant to give that up, despite knowing what it costs in terms of the rest of my life." He went on to talk about the conflict between thought and action. "I like to think that I could really do it, and that's hard to let go of. But there actually is a difference between a daydream and an action plan. I shouldn't be so scared of the daydream that I have to shut down my mind, but I'd better watch when I get swept up in the excitement of a plan."

Closed-system functioning always remains a potential for both patient and analyst. Under stress, old anxieties, beliefs and reactions characteristic of the closed system can be expected. By the termination phase, open-system functioning, evidenced in accomplishment of therapeutic alliance tasks and the availability of alternative responses to stress, is at peak efficiency. But the reality of ending also intensifies the potential for closed-system, omnipotent responses in both people. Mr. Q experienced that pull, but used the skills developed in his treatment to notice, and imagine monitoring himself in the future. Working with a two-system model kept me aware that closed-system solutions would always be available, and protected me from discouragement at their recurrence. I could validate Mr. Q's perceptions and reinforce his sense that he would always have to be mindful of his alternatives. He now had the freedom to choose his response.

Mrs. T

In her struggles over her sadness, Mrs. T would slide into self-pity, presenting herself once again as a helpless person, with the omnipotent belief that she could force me to keep her after all if she were a mess. She also described herself as "depressed" whenever she was angry at the constraints of reality, particularly at the inexorable progress of time toward the termination date. Mrs. T again began to have daydreams of starting an illicit relationship with a man at work, who from her descriptions sounded like a sadistic, controlling person. I pointed out that she was contemplating continuing a relationship of power and control and wondered what she felt would happen if she gave up that pattern of interaction with others. "Somebody has to be in charge!" Mrs. T exploded.

Several days of intense anger and anxiety followed her outburst. She telephoned me, saying that she thought she should be put on medication. I noted that her presentation of herself as incompetent had not pushed me to change the termination date, so she seemed to have upped the ante with her insistence that her feelings were so powerful that no one could control them. It seemed like a temper tantrum. I remarked on how she was using her feelings to bully and control, as she had with her parents. This comment brought her back to earlier work, when Mrs. T had remembered her parents describing the "awful tantrums" she had when she was a toddler, and talking about how helpless they felt in the face of her feelings. Overwhelmed by anxiety and rage from the inside, she had been met by equally overwhelmed grownups; she was thrown on her own resources to deal with her feelings, and developed omnipotent beliefs in her capacity to use them to control others. I remarked how those beliefs might have seemed like the only available avenue at the time and wondered what had made Mrs. T feel equally resourceless in the present. Mrs. T laughed and said, "It's the same old stuff – there are no guarantees and I really do wish I could have a warranty." This brought us both back into the real present of the treatment and our working relationship, and turned our joint attention to Mrs. T's actual future ideas about what she could rely on after treatment.

NEGOTIATING INTENSE CONFLICT BETWEEN
THE TWO SYSTEMS/CONTINUED DEFENSE ANALYSIS

The reality of ending confronts the denial of change, time, reality constraints and the inability to control another that is characteristic of closed-system functioning. Mr. G picked a date and our termination phase began. By the end of the first week, he mounted a major effort to get me to go back on our agreement, do away with the ending date, or at least defer it for a year. It was a powerful effort, including a weekend of binge drinking and drugs, sexual bullying of his wife, and threats to fire his entire staff. He insisted that these events proved I was wrong, that he was not ready to finish, and maybe never would be.

I worried briefly to myself about whether I had been mistaken about his readiness to finish and then, thinking in two-systems terms about closed-system manifestations as solutions, I wondered out loud about the function of his furor. Did the extreme intensity indicate that he was back to fighting off the painful task of setting aside his belief that he could use his troubles to force me to do his bidding? Mr. G sighed and said he had always hated change as a child. He turned every routine into an unalterable ritual, and now analysis has become that protective ritual he couldn't do without. With therapy he would never grow old, get sick, or die; with me he could imagine that he was still young and slim with a full head of hair. On his own Mr. G realized that the ending date was a confrontation with his closed-system omnipotent beliefs, and then he was able to experience the ending date as a helpful anchor point.

One way to conceptualize the fluctuations of the termination phase is in terms of more consistent open-system functioning interspersed with flareups of closed-system defensive reactions. Over the following weeks, Mr. G tried to provoke me to become more active. He claimed he couldn't think, associate, or recall anything, and asserted that I knew everything anyway. Perceiving not only the attribution of his ego functions to me, but also the externalization of his conviction about his own omnipotence, I remarked that he wasn't really setting aside his omnipotent beliefs. He was just handing the power over to me, while secretly retaining the idea that he could force me to use that power. Mr. G recalled a childhood religious phase when he believed he had special prayers that could force God to do his specific bidding.

Mr. G's forcing of his fetishistic sexual acts on women had come up at many points during the treatment, with Mr. G trying to get me to forbid these practices. In the termination phase, after he had failed to get me to change the date, Mr. G escalated his provocations. He began to tease and humiliate his younger son quite brutally. I asked him why, when he had all the skills to direct his own analysis and his own life, he was trying to force me to intervene actively, for instance, by calling children's protective services.

Mr. G was shocked. He hadn't realized how far he had gone. He said, "I'm having a temper tantrum. I don't want to work, be responsible, grow up. It's some kind of fantasy, it's worse, it's a delusion that I can control the world by being a boorish, sadistic, shouting asshole. I truly believe it when I'm doing it. I feel strong and powerful, but look what I almost did to my son and my family and my analysis." He began to cry. "I love my son and yet I was willing to destroy him to hang on to this craziness." From this point on, Mr. G stopped externalizing on to me, and began to allow himself to feel sadness and mourn the imminent loss of his analysis and of me.

We weathered this stormy passage with the assistance of two-systems thinking on my part. Reminding myself that closed-system defenses are invoked as self-protection when a person feels threatened with trauma helped me retain sympathy and empathy when

Mr. G was behaving in a nasty way not seen since the early months of his treatment. Being mindful of my own internal closed-system pull to gratification at being idealized and put back up on a pedestal of knowledge and skill kept me clear about the reality of Mr. G's well-practiced open-system capacities. Holding on to that part of my therapeutic role that involves standing for reality, for open-system facts, helped me set a limit when I was hearing about abusive behavior that could not be allowed to continue.

DISAPPOINTMENT IN BOTH OPEN AND CLOSED SYSTEMS

A two-systems model allows us to differentiate admiration, which functions in the open system, and idealization, which is a hostile, closed-system, omnipotent attempt to deny real imperfections and failings of important people (parents, analyst). Omnipotent ideas are not aimed at enhancing the real qualities of the self or other, but rather at denying and transforming pain in the parent-child relationship, filling the gap between the inadequate and the good-enough parent. Disappointment and disillusionment can arise in the context of maintaining closed-system idealized expectations, or can be part of realistic deidealization as a result of addressing those closed-system defenses and accepting reality.

Mr. M

Mr. M had a very long treatment and eventually set a termination date for a few months ahead. He began one week shaking with rage as he expressed his need to control and boss. "The moral is I can provide for myself, but the wish is you'll do it for me. I'll break down at the bottom of the street. You'll see me and you'll come and give me the best pep talk I've ever heard. The rescue will make all the angry feelings go away. You're not the depressed, incompetent mother. Look at what you can do and you're doing it for me!"

Then he went back to talking about the flaws he perceived in me. "Seeing your imperfections derails me. You work too hard. If you were my father, I'd be afraid to invite my friends home because you'd always be busy. I am responsible for how you are.

We're back into my feelings of shame and responsibility. Why can't I accept your imperfection? So you're not Mickey Mantle or Willy Mays – so what?" Mr. M was able to work out for himself what was going on, but we could also think together about the ways in which the pressure of his feelings and his holding on to an omnipotent belief that their intensity could make me rescue him was a perennial tension whenever he felt sad.

Mr. L

Disappointment also belongs in the open system, as part of coming to terms with reality. Mr. L started a long treatment as a young man in a state of acute panic, preoccupied with the fear that he had cancer or syphilis, paralyzed in terms of progressive movement in life or work. Frequently confused or disoriented, he felt he had lost his grip on reality. He constantly worried that his penis would be cut by a razor. Mr. L was the second son of Holocaust survivors and, during the first years of treatment, he attempted to live out his fantasies of the Holocaust experience. He alternated between being the oppressed victim and the Nazi sadist. When the patient had been 6 months old, his father had died and his mother had smuggled him and his brother across borders into Western Europe. Much of the analysis focused on his search for his dead father, and his wishes and fears that surviving him represented an unacceptable triumph. Mr. L felt he had no right to a life as an adult man.

Toward the end of his analysis, Mr. L talked about the changes that had taken place; from his point of view, there were many satisfactory ones. He enjoyed his work; he had courted and married a suitable woman; they had bought a house and planned a family. He was comfortable with himself and had plans for the future. But, he remarked, "I am leaving without being different. I have the energy now for my wife, my work and the child who will come. But I am not cured of myself. This is what I wanted; this is why I came into analysis. I always wanted to be someone else. The whole original purpose of coming here was to be castrated, to be removed from myself, so now I am relieved, but I realize I am disappointed and sad to leave those thoughts behind." With my continued articulation of the contrast between omnipotent beliefs in being able to rewrite history, or change his father's destiny, and the real open-system possibilities in the present and future, he was coming to terms with how long and hard he had held on to his closed-system beliefs and how difficult it was to set them aside.

Mrs. T

With Mrs. T, we could see that, throughout her treatment, there was a struggle within her between the wish to hold on to past patterns of sadomasochistic relationships that represented closed-system solutions with hope of magical gratification and the progressive open-system forces that represented realistic relations with others and the world, mediated by competent functioning and yielding genuine, predictable pleasure. Focus on the therapeutic alliance tasks at each phase allowed for the emergence and consolidation of an alternate open system of self-regulation. Setting aside her closed-system solutions from all levels of development, including magical omnipotent images of perfection in herself and others, seemed a frightening and painful loss.

But the work of the earlier phases really established alternative sources of security and self-esteem in realistic achievements and representations. Much of the work of the termination phase involved drawing the distinction between the illusory loss of unreal fantasy gains and the real loss of the setting, the unique therapeutic relationship, and me. We had first talked about this when she imagined me disappearing from being blasted into space. The hostile wishes contained in her fears and the underlying omnipotent beliefs were worked through repeatedly. Such fears resurfaced in the face of the reality of ending.

Mrs. T oscillated between comfort in staying with the reality of the imminent end and fantasies about ways she could get me to change myself, the date, or the relationship. A week before the termination date, she seemed low-keyed and somewhat quieter than usual. "I'd like to write a different ending to this story," she remarked. I recalled how much we had learned from the characters in the stories she wrote and wondered how she would understand a character who tried so hard to redesign the world. Mrs. T snapped back, "I don't need a character to know I can't stand disappointment!" Then she said, "I really surprised myself with that. I guess it was waiting there to come out, but I have been fighting it off. Maybe that's why I've been feeling so subdued." She went on to examine the idea of being disappointed and faced her feeling that I had not been the perfect mother she always wished for, nor was she herself ever going to be the perfect person she had for so long striven to be. "Maybe now, though, I won't have to run off and have affairs to let myself know that what I really feel is all right."

LOVE AT TERMINATION

Dr. X had chosen a date about three months ahead, and the first month of the termination phase was marked by intensive reworking of old conflicts over loss. Working through intense feelings about his mother and his former therapist allowed him to regain and consolidate a feeling of objective love for himself and me. Then he began to talk of his postanalytic plans, both professional and personal. At first this seemed an appropriate and progressive open-system step. Gradually, however, the sessions became filled with ruminations about what he should do in regard to this or that hypothetical postanalytic occurrence. Should he seek an academic hospital post, should he take it, what about his patients, and so forth. The present experience of termination seemed to have been swallowed up in concerns about the future.

During Dr. X's sessions, I too found myself drifting into the future, joining him in discussing his putative postanalytic conflicts. I then noticed that I seemed to have lost some loving feeling for him in the present. One evening I was rereading an article by Judith Viorst about the fantasies of analysts during the termination phase.[109] I had used her material in a number of my own papers, and I thought I was going over it for a course I was preparing. I made no connection with my patient, until I found myself thinking repeatedly about Viorst's report of an analyst who fantasized that his patient would meet and marry the analyst's grown-up child. I wondered then if that was my wish for an altered relationship after the analysis. Dr. X and I would stay together as father and son.

I was not only avoiding my own sadness and allowing him to avoid his; I had also relinquished my objective love for him as an autonomous. accomplished person who no longer needed me. I had a fantasy that might have seemed benign and loving, but it was actually an omnipotent desire to control my patient's future. In the next session, I said that we both seemed to be working very hard to avoid our feelings about ending. Dr. X sighed and said that he realized he was trying to leave me in a way he had always left everyone – without any feelings of love or sadness or loss. He went on to say that his treatment provided him a chance to leave while loving and feeling loved. "It would be sad," he said, "but sad is better than dead, and there is no sadness without love."

21

Post-Termination

LIFE AFTER TREATMENT

Post-termination is not strictly speaking a phase of treatment, but much of the work of therapy is shaped by its goals and measured by the quality of life afterward. Therapy is a means to reach the goal of freedom to choose, to restoration to the path of progressive development, to re-immersion in the river of time and reality, not an end in itself. Implicitly the entire treatment has been a preparation for post-termination living.

THERAPEUTIC TASK: LIVING AND CREATIVITY

Reflecting on this open-ended time period from our two-systems perspective gives rise to a number of propositions.

- Our view is that conflict is ubiquitous and universal. Closed- and open-system solutions remain a potential throughout life. Thus treatment never obliterates closed-system solutions; both therapist and patient have the potential to choose closed-system responses at times of stress.

- Change and transformation also persist throughout life, and thus open-system responses may become newly available at any point.
- The therapeutic relationship is unique in both people's lives. This is an open-system perception of a real fact. Therefore it is important to retain its possibilities after treatment formally ends. That means the analyst remains the person's analyst forever, maintaining the therapeutic stance, despite internal or external pressures to alter the relationship. Continuing positive growth after treatment is only possible when there is continuity between the time of analysis and afterward.
- In practical terms, that possibility is often realized by patients' writing to let their therapist know how their self-analytic work has proceeded, or returning for a "top-up" or "tune-up" if they have hit a snag.
- A two-systems model allows for both therapist and patient to experience a return to treatment as an open-system manifestation of the person taking good care of themselves, rather than a failure, an attack or a humiliation.

CLINICAL EXAMPLES

GROWTH CONTINUES

Mr. C

Mr. C, who had first protested "No way!" in dismay when I had offered the idea during the termination phase that he would become a better analyst to himself than I was, sent a letter a few months after the end of treatment. He wrote about a puzzling piece of his history that he solved through working on a dream and then confirmed with his only surviving relative. He learned that, as an infant, he had been shipped out to his grandmother for a few months while his parents took an extended trip to Europe. "In the past I would have used the discovery to lord it over you, to exclaim that I could do something you couldn't do. But I don't feel that way. I am enormously grateful for the work we did together and for you equipping and allowing me to keep going. It took the full experience of our good-bye to access all the earlier goodbyes."

Mr. L

Mr. L, the child of Holocaust survivors whose father died when he was an infant, left treatment pleased about the changes in his life, but immensely sad that he was still himself. He wrote to me two-and-a-half years later: "The analytic process continued very actively for many months after the analysis and it is only recently that I feel I have reached the natural conclusion of it as a distinct part of my life and as a distinct method of investigation of problems."

Mr. L described thinking about the image of a child on a flinty road trying to catch up with a man who may or may not be his father. He described how, in the course of his self-analysis, he realized the whole point of the image was never to catch up with his father, to seek out failure, because failure meant pursuit, but never catching up. Never catching up meant his father is not dead – he's there, ahead somewhere. He wrote that it took years after the treatment to assimilate me, not analysis, as a failure. It was only through experiencing my failure – my limitations, my inability to fulfill his intense longing for reunion with his father – that he could gradually accept his own limitations and finally set aside the wish to constantly chase after but always deny the death of his father.

Mr. L was able to set aside his closed-system omnipotent belief in his capacity to keep himself safe by keeping his father alive, forged in childhood in response to situations of extreme helplessness, with application of the open-system skills forged in treatment and internalized throughout.

RETURNING TO TREATMENT AS AN OPEN-SYSTEM CHOICE

Mr. Q had worked very hard and successfully in his treatment. He subsequently married and had children. His wife then plunged into a serious depression, which did not seem to respond to either medication or therapy. Mr. Q first recontacted me for some suggestions about that situation, which was making him feel helpless. He then said that he really should come in himself, since he had begun feeling surges of frustrated fury at his wife and he was worried that he would actually do something harmful to the family.

In the termination phase, we not only talk in general about post-termination phenomena, but anticipate with patients their particular closed-system vulnerabilities, for instance, Mr. Q's propensity for impulsive or violent solutions. This is part of open-system clearsightedness in encompassing the reality that closed-system solutions are never truly eradicated. When Mr. Q resumed therapy, he remembered that we had talked about his potential to react this way to helpless frustration. It comforted him that we shared the understanding that, even in the midst of a rage, he needn't act on it, but had another choice. He could call me and together we would figure out an alternative solution, as we had done many times before.

Contacting the therapist again because of difficulties is in itself an open-system act. It demonstrates the exercise of the capacity to choose to take good care of oneself. That helps therapists to resist the pull to closed-system masochistic feelings of failure and depression when patients seem to relapse. Mental health professionals have a high rate of burnout and suicide. We think that recasting the goals of treatment in terms of restoration of the capacity to choose between two systems of self-regulation has profound impact on how therapists can see their work. Every interaction with patients generates data for assessing progress on this dimension of change. Having a choice is something every patient, of any age, can understand, first as a goal, then gradually as an experience, and both are shared with the therapist. This goal touches on profound human issues, but is not overambitious or omnipotent, since the potential capacity for creating alternatives and making a genuine choice is there in all patients and all therapists.

Afterword

This brief volume summarizes the main assumptions, findings, and applications of our two-systems model. But, as we noted earlier, a theory or model is only a fiction, a heuristic trope that is more or less useful to help us make sense of and negotiate the complex domains of phenomena. It is measured by its usefulness rather than its truth.

As a reminder of the limitations of particular methods we should remember that the most powerful cure for all emotional ailments is the placebo effect. A therapist's belief in the method he uses will produce positive change in 50% of his clients. Given those realities we have to ask where we have arrived and where we would like to go.

We can say that our own clinical work and that of our students has seemed significantly more effective and successful as we used the two-systems model to expand the domain, to include as psychoanalytic many concepts and techniques that had been discarded, such as the therapeutic alliance, and to explicitly include human qualities of care, concern and objective love as essential to the process of growth and change.

But these positive results can be validated only by us and our students and colleagues. An objective change related to our open-system acknowledgement of reality and our emphasis on the developmental point of view is including parents fully in our analyses of children and adolescents. Most child analysts now do so[110] and we suggest that adult-only analysts may benefit from attention to the reactions of significant others when they work with their adult patients. Many experienced adult analysts actually do think about these issues, but have no theoretical backing for looking beyond the static world of the transference/countertransference of closed-system intrapsychic functioning. Closed-system omnipotent beliefs have been reliably measured in a parenting scale we developed,[111] in Rorschach responses,[112] and in the authoritarian personality scale referred to earlier in this book.[113] This points to the possibility of measuring changes in Open/Closed-system functioning in empirical research on therapeutic growth and outcome.

We have found that a two-system model gives us the freedom to justify and ground an expanded range of techniques; it allows us to articulate explicitly the purpose and effect of interventions analysts may ordinarily take for granted or not know how to talk comfortably about, without having to postulate a paradigm shift.

We have also found that the two-systems model and the alternatives inherent in this formulation encouraged us to listen more closely to the language we used with patients, colleagues and the public. We believe that the model gives us a basis to develop ways of talking and writing which are immediate and relevant to the general population, as Freud's German style was to people at the beginning of the 20th century. Our work in schools and our book on Emotional Muscle are efforts in that direction, as we seek accessible, experience-near, evocative descriptions.

We have developed an ever-expanding list of what we have called "distinguishables." Originating probably in our earliest work together on differentiating projection and externalization, we've become interested in psychoanalytic and general concepts that are confounded, conflated, or just plain confused and confusing. Sorting out the connections with closed- and open-system functioning has served to generate powerful interpretative and conceptual tools to the benefit of our patients, students and ourselves. Some of these are discussed in various theoretical papers, some in our clinical descriptions, some in the application of the two-systems model to education and community work, and some point us to future directions of inquiry. (A sample list follows the section on Novick Two Systems Writings.)

The confluence of our emphasis on the developmental underpinnings of psychoanalytic thinking with our insights about the operationalizing of a two-systems model in working with sadomasochistic omnipotent functioning and the therapeutic alliance has application to issues of training in our field. One result of our efforts is the increasing adoption of integrated child and adult training curricula in centers nationally and internationally. We also try to offer an alternative to an ever-narrowing definition of psychoanalysis as confined solely to transference/countertransference interactions based on projective identifications. The two-systems model leads us back to psychoanalysis as a general psychology of normal and pathological development and functioning, the most comprehensive theory currently available. Then we can describe psychoanalytic treatment as a developmentally-informed, strength-based, multimodal technique.

People are not simple and the reality of their lives is challenging in myriad ways. There is tremendous cultural and financial pressure to find quick, easy fixes for what are actually complex situations. And a corresponding pressure for quick, easy gratifications to assuage feelings of powerlessness. We would now characterize these as closed-system, omnipotent solutions and trace their roots as we have done in the previous chapters.

Only a theory and flexible models that honor and encompass complexity and the almost infinite variety of available choices and solutions in response to life's joys and sorrows can do justice to the needs of people of all ages who seek our help.

We suggest that our evolving two-systems model is one way to help individuals achieve the freedom to choose how they want to live their lives. There is much work still to do and we hope that readers will join us in the ongoing endeavor.

Novick Two Systems Writings

This section consists of a selected annotated bibliography of our published and unpublished writings relevant to the two-systems model. We include these here in chronological order to trace the evolution of our ideas and the various component concepts and applications, as well as to offer the reader some indications of what the more detailed content and discussion of each original source includes.

PROJECTION AND EXTERNALIZATION (1970)

Novick, J. and Kelly, K. (1970) Projection and externalization. Psychoanalytic Study of The Child 25: 69-95

This is the first of our joint papers. In it we explore the long history and complexity of these foundational concepts and offer distinctions which seem clinically useful. In our later expositions of closed-system functioning we see externalization as a major defense of the closed system. In this paper we discuss the impact of adult externalizations on to children, externalization of responsibility, externalization of aspects of the self, and externalization of the drives or "projection proper."

We questioned the use of projection as a portmanteau term covering everything from neonatal development to artistic expression in order to emphasize the clinical importance of distinguishing among the various types of externalizations and the differential impact on the person who is the object of externalizations. For example, we provide clinical illustrations of the different kinds of damage done to children's developing personalities when they are used by parents as carriers of devalued parts of the parents or as targets for projections.

BEATING FANTASIES IN CHILDREN (1972)

Novick, J., Novick, K.K. (1972). Beating Fantasies in Children. Int. J. Psycho-Anal., 53: 237-242
Reprinted in: Fearful Symmetry 1996, Chapter 1

This paper was the first in the long line of our work on sadomasochism and two systems of self-regulation. Our interest in this topic came first from our wish to understand the problems in treating especially difficult child and adolescent patients at the Anna Freud Centre (then the Hampstead Clinic) in the 1960's. When we looked at the records of the most problematic treatments, it became clear that each case showed evidence of a beating fantasy. Through seeking to understand Freud's statement that the beating fantasy is the "essence of masochism" (1919, p.189), we undertook a study of the development of beating fantasies in children, which then led to our describing a sequence of organizing fantasies in development.

We concluded that a beating fantasy is often a normal transitional component of postoedipal development in girls and may be quite common, serving, among others, the function of establishing the difference between receptivity and passivity.

In contrast to the girls with this transitory beating fantasy, we found children and adults, male and female, with a "fixed beating fantasy," which is a relatively permanent, organizing part of the individual's psychosexual life, and occurs in the context of severe pathology with accompanying ego disturbances and problems of self-esteem regulation. This is a crucial difference and important to the discussion of sadism, as our findings about the occurrence of beating fantasies in a normal and a pathological form, with such substantive differences between them, suggested that we consider the development of these phenomena in a different way. This led eventually to the formulation of the two-systems model.

NEGATIVE THERAPEUTIC MOTIVATION AND NEGATIVE THERAPEUTIC ALLIANCE (1980)

Novick, J. (1980). Negative therapeutic motivation and negative therapeutic alliance. Psychoanal. Study Child, 35: 299 – 320
Reprinted in: Fearful Symmetry 1996, chapter 12

This paper is a study of treatment failures, an effort to understand and suggest explanations and remedies. With clinical illustrations and discussions of technique we demonstrate that the alliance is not only a positive force, but can also become a vehicle for externalizing parental failure on to the therapist. This was an early example of technical approaches to grappling with the challenges of closed-system family dynamics where externalization played a pivotal role.

VARIETIES OF TRANSFERENCE IN THE ANALYSIS OF AN ADOLESCENT (1982)

Novick, J. (1982). Varieties of transference in the analysis of an adolescent. Int. J. Psycho – Anal. 63: 139 – 148.
Reprinted in: Fearful Symmetry 1996, chapter 6

Following on our earlier study of externalization we here focus on the "externalizing transference." This is based on externalizing a part of the self on to the therapist in contrast to a "differentiated transference" where the analyst is seen as a separate person colored by past or current relationships.

ATTEMPTED SUICIDE IN ADOLESCENCE: THE SUICIDE SEQUENCE (1984)

Novick, J. (1984). Attempted suicide in adolescence: the suicide sequence. In: Suicide in the Young. Ed. Sudak, H.S., Ford, A.B., Rushforth, N.B. Boston, MA: John Wright, P.S.G. Inc.: 524 – 548. Reprinted in: Essential Papers on Suicide. Ed. J. Maltsberger and M. Goldblatt. New York, New York Universities Press, 1996, 524 – 528. Reprinted in Fearful Symmetry 1996, Chapter 8

This paper, which is informed by study of 84 adolescents who presented to a walk-in clinic after medically serious suicide attempts, focal research on 7 of those adolescents who were seen in psychoanalysis, and cross validation of the findings with a further case of a near fatal suicide attempt by an adolescent led to postulating a sequence of steps (we isolated 10) typically leading to the actual attempt. In each case the actual attempt followed failure to transform the mother/child relationship, with rage displaced from mother to another (including the therapist) and the belief that suicide is a brave, magical act that will change everyone. It always included the idea that they will die but not die and be around to see the impact of their omnipotent act on others.

This experience and clinical work with other such patients contributed to our views on sadomasochism and the centrality of omnipotent beliefs, and form part of the roots of our two-systems model.

THE ESSENCE OF MASOCHISM (1987)

Novick, K.K. & Novick, J. (1987). The essence of masochism. Psychoanalytic Study of the Child 42: 353- 384

This paper contains our main ideas about the closed, sadomasochistic system and how it evolves through developmental phases from birth to adulthood. After examining a series of child, adolescent, and adult cases we suggested defining masochism as follows: "Masochism is the active pursuit of psychic or physical pain, suffering, or humiliation in the service of adaptation, defense, and instinctual gratification at oral, anal, and phallic levels." We go on to say, "In our view, not only are derivatives of each phase discernible in masochism, but the pain-seeking behavior which starts in infancy alters and is altered by each subsequent phase, including the oedipal and post-oedipal. Postoedipally, masochistic impulses are organized as conscious or unconscious fantasies that are fixed, resistant to modification by experience or analysis, serve multiple ego functions, and take the form, although not necessarily the content, of the beating fantasy. In the fantasies the subject is an innocent victim, who achieves through suffering reunion with the object, defense against aggressive destruction and loss of the object, avoidance of narcissistic pain, and instinctual gratification by fantasy participation in the oedipal situation. Suicidal pathology, masochistic perversions, certain forms of hypochondriasis and psychosomatic illness, and moral masochism have in common an *underlying fantasy structure*. In our view, this fantasy structure is the 'essence of masochism' (Freud 1919, p. 189)."

SOME COMMENTS ON MASOCHISM AND THE DELUSION OF OMNIPOTENCE (1991)

Novick, J. and Novick, K.K. (1991) Some comments on masochism and the delusion of omnipotence from a developmental perspective. J.A.P.A. 39: 307 -331.

Here we trace the epigenetic development of omnipotent fantasies (we now call these beliefs) and we demonstrate with clinical material the relationship between the pain-seeking behavior of sadomasochism and the consolidation of an omnipotent belief. It is in this paper that we begin to explore two systems of self-regulation and the application of these ideas to technique.

POST-OEDIPAL TRANSFORMATIONS: LATENCY, ADOLESCENCE, AND PATHOGENESIS (1994)

Novick, K.K. and Novick, J. (1994). Post-Oedipal transformations: latency, adolescence and pathogenesis. J.A.P.A. 42: 143-170

This paper questions the assumption that pathogenesis resides only or mainly in the very early mother/infant period. Using cases from all developmental levels we suggest that "the past transforms and is transformed by the present." We conclude that "we can never know the past directly." But a knowledge of the transformations appropriate to each phase, from infancy to adulthood, gives us additional access to the determinants and functions of the patient's pathology in the present, increases the specificity of genetic interpretation, and gives the patient and analyst greater conviction about the accuracy of the essential work of reconstruction.

Here we see the roots of our views, expressed in later papers and in this book, on "open-system reconstruction."

EXTERNALIZATION AS A PATHOLOGICAL FORM OF RELATING: THE DYNAMIC UNDERPINNINGS OF ABUSE (1994)

Novick, J. and Novick, K.K. (1994). Externalization as a pathological form of relating: the dynamic underpinnings of abuse. In. Victims of Abuse. Ed. A. Sugarman et al. Madison, CT: I.U.P. Press, pp. 45 – 68.
Reprinted in: Fearful Symmetry 1996, Chapter 7

Building on the formulations of our 1970 paper on projection and externalization we use material from the cases of a preschool child, an adolescent, and an adult, who were each sexually abused by family members, to assert that externalization is an abuse in itself and is a condition which allows for sexual or physical abuse.

In this paper we establish externalization (bolstered by denial and turning the aggression against the self) as a major mechanism of the closed system. Such defense mechanisms are transmitted through the generations, from parent to child.

A DEVELOPMENTAL PERSPECTIVE ON OMNIPOTENCE (1996)

Novick, J. and Novick, K.K. (1996). A developmental perspective on omnipotence. J. Clinical Psychoanalysis. 5: 124 – 173

This is an extension of our views on omnipotence, integrated at this point with the work of Leon Wurmser. We again emphasize our difference from the classical Ferenczi view of omnipotence as normal, given up and mourned in response to ordinary reality. We assert here that omnipotence is a hostile defense generated at any point in development in response to the failure of reality to meet ordinary needs.

"I WON'T DANCE": A PSYCHOANALYTIC PERSPECTIVE ON INTERFERENCES WITH PERFORMANCE (1996)

Novick, K.K. and Novick, J. (1996). I won't dance: a psychoanalytic approach to interferences with performance. Unpublished manuscript.

These three linked papers were originally written for the Lucy Daniels Foundation (Cary, North Carolina) annual symposium on Creativity and Psychoanalysis. They include detailed case material, illustrative film clips, and, on that original occasion, intervals of live performance by artists of various kinds, followed by discussion.

We framed the ideas as an exploration of the relationships among the artist, the performer, and the audience, bringing a two-systems developmental perspective to bear on

I.   Omnipotence in Infancy and Early Childhood
II. Omnipotence in Childhood, Adolescence and Adulthood.

We began with the idea that there are performance elements in all aspects of life. In looking developmentally at performance, we noted that the first audience for the first performance for every one of us is a mother. We discuss the forces that conduce to omnipotent interactions between child and parents, as well as those that nurture creativity and health. We looked at the developmental strands from each phase of childhood as they appear in adult pathology. We particularly emphasized the importance of late adolescent development for consolidating closed-system functioning or offering another chance to set omnipotence aside and move into creative, generative adulthood, with mutually-enhancing relationships with others.

III. A Painter, a Poet, a Dancer, a Musician, and an Architect – Performance Conflicts and Resolutions

Then we traced the interactions and conflicts between open-system and closed-system functioning, looking at interferences with performance in both successful and aspiring artists, noting that artists and performers are particularly vulnerable to the shift from an illusion of a wished-for or pretended omnipotence to a delusional conviction of omnipotence.

In addition to the constant challenge and stress of performance there are further factors that contribute to the particular vulnerability of artists and performers. These are the role played by performers as receivers and conveyors of cultural fantasies, the special childhoods of performers, and the collusion of the audience. These aspects are also examined in relation to Adolf Hitler as a performer on the world stage.

THE REALITY OF HITLER AND THE DELUSION OF OMNIPOTENCE (1996)

Novick, J., Novick, K.K., and Novick, B.Z.
The Reality of Hitler and the Delusion of Omnipotence
Unpublished. Available upon request.

There are two distinct views on the development, vicissitudes, pathology, and potential virulence of omnipotent fantasies. The classical psychoanalytic description stems mainly from Ferenczi. This position holds that omnipotence is part of normal development and that fantasies of omnipotence are given up when they are contradicted by reality. The fantasies themselves are considered benign, as captured in Freud's image of the infant, held securely in his mother's arms, surrounded by adoring adults, as "His Majesty the baby." This assumption has profound implications for theories of child development and for therapeutic technique.

In contrast, we have presented the view that omnipotent beliefs constitute the destructive core of sadomasochism, and can emerge as a pathological solution to experiences of failure of reality to meet basic ego needs at every stage of development. A delusion of omnipotence is a hostile defense against helplessness, an organizing view of the self which becomes ever more complex and self-fulfilling with each developmental failure. It is finally consolidated at adolescence as the core fantasy of a sadomasochistic engagement with people and the world.

Readily available facts of Adolf Hitler's life are used in this paper to illustrate a number of the points in our formulations about omnipotence. This allows also for suggesting a different perspective on some historical questions about Hitler's pathology, his relation to the German people, to reality, and the reasons for some of his decisions.

PANEL CONTRIBUTION ON
FEMALE PERVERSION (1996)

Novick, J. and Novick, K.K. Panel Contribution after presentation by Louise Kaplan, Ph.D to Michigan Society of Psychoanalytic Psychology, November 9, 1996
Unpublished. Available on request.

This discussion was an application of the two-systems model to four of the areas in which we suggested that female perversion can be seen. The first was that of pathological use of the body, particularly in adolescence. We discussed attempted suicide in adolescence as an illustration, as this occurs 10 to 20 times more frequently in female than in male teenagers (males complete many more suicides). Analysis of teenagers who have survived serious suicide attempts has revealed a sadomasochistic central fantasy, what we would now characterize as a closed-system defense. Second were some dating patterns in later adolescence. The format of certain long-term relationships was the third. And the fourth, often unnoticed or hidden, certainly underaddressed, can reside in patterns of parenting.

The forms of perversion may appear different in men and women but we think the dynamics are the same. The roots of perverse functioning are found in each phase of development, starting with pathological fantasies in pregnancy, which cross the generational barrier to affect the earliest development of the individual.

FEARFUL SYMMETRY: THE DEVELOPMENT AND
TREATMENT OF SADOMASOCHISM (1996)

Paperback 2007
Novick, J. & Novick, K.K. (1996). Fearful Symmetry: The Development and Treatment of Sadomasochism. Northvale, NJ: Jason Aronson

Available from Amazon, the publisher, or directly from the authors

In the introduction we note that despite many changes in our thinking since we started publishing our work, there are four consistent and interlocking themes that we discern.

1) The necessity for a multidimensional or metapsychological approach to all psychological phenomena; 2) the importance of the developmental point of view; 3) an assumption that child and adolescent analytic material and observations of infants and children have much to contribute to the understanding and technique of working with adults; and 4) a conviction that sadomasochistic power relations and delusions of omnipotence are part of the core of all pathology.

Integrating these 4 themes led us to posit a two-systems model of self-regulation and apply the model both to theory and an expansion of technique. This book serves as the foundation for our work in the following 20 years, encompassing the ideas that led, for instance, to the establishment of an integrated child/adult curriculum nationally and internationally, the theoretical foundation for expanding our work with children and adolescents by including concurrent parent work, the founding of Allen Creek Preschool, an award winning psychoanalytic preschool for children and parents, the founding of the Alliance for Psychoanalytic Schools, establishing the importance of pre-termination and termination phases of treatment, and expansion of the concept of the therapeutic alliance.

EGO DISRUPTION IN AN ABUSED LITTLE GIRL (1997)

Novick, K.K. (1997). Ego disruption in an abused little girl. Psychoanal. Inq. 17: 3, 267 – 285

Expanded version published in Fearful Symmetry 1996, Chapter 9

A case presentation of a sexually abused little girl who started treatment at age 5, published in an issue of the journal devoted to sexual abuse. Fascinating in itself, this report also illustrates how memories are transformed, challenges us to define trauma beyond the specific event, and illustrates the destructive impact of parental externalizations. Those three aspects of the case are relevant to thinking about the cognitive and emotional interferences that result from closed-system functioning in parents and child.

NOT FOR BARBARIANS: AN APPRECIATION OF FREUD'S "A CHILD IS BEING BEATEN" (1997)

Novick, J. & Novick, K.K. (1997). Not for barbarians: an appreciation of Freud's "a child is being beaten." In: E. Person, P. Fonagy, and S. Figuera (Eds.) On Freud's "A child is being beaten." New Haven, CT: Yale University Press. 1997, pp. 31-46

We note here that many analysts ignore Freud's paper on beating fantasies, but we value this paper as answering many questions about the riddle of sadomasochism. In particular we see his work as pointing toward a developmental understanding of the transformations of memory and desire from infancy to adolescence. He also places the motive for the beating fantasy in what we would now call the domain of self-regulation, with the beating fantasy being a closed-system way of dealing with shame and an attempt to restore omnipotent beliefs. In the paper we also note that Freud omitted the role of the pre-oedipal mother in the formation of sadomasochism, as did Anna Freud in her later paper on beating fantasies.

AN APPLICATION OF THE CONCEPT OF THE THERAPEUTIC ALLIANCE TO SADOMASOCHISTIC PATHOLOGY (1998)

Novick, K.K. and Novick, J. (1998). An application of the concept of the therapeutic alliance to sadomasochistic pathology. JAPA 46:813 -846

This paper presents the history of the therapeutic alliance, the extrusion of this technical concept from psychoanalysis, the adoption of this concept by adjoining fields, and demonstrates how robust this concept is in predicting positive change. We present a revised theory of the alliance, incorporating the contributions of many and correcting what we think were the unhelpful views of some.

The revised alliance theory posits a series of common sense tasks for patient, analyst and significant others at each phase of treatment. A single case is followed through the phases and the work is summarized as follows:

"Grappling with the tasks of the therapeutic alliance at each phase of treatment restored to 'Mrs. T' her potential for adaptive transformation. From accomplishing the alliance task of 'being with another' came confidence in her capacity to be alone with herself, to value herself, and to cooperate in a trusting, mutually enhancing relationship with others. She could use a new level and range of ego functions activated in working together with the analyst for creative, joyful living and for self-analysis when necessary. The skill of self-analysis was developed in the context of a focus on independent therapeutic work. Setting aside magical infantile fantasy solutions strengthened Mrs. T's competent, reality-attuned mode of self-regulation. The capacities restored and the tools forged in the accomplishment of these therapeutic alliance tasks equipped Mrs. T for her lifelong struggle against the potential to resolve conflicts with sadomasochistic fantasies."

Thus the paper traces shifts in the patient's functioning from the predominant use of closed-system methods to confidence in the exercise of open-system capacities.

WHAT ARE YOU GOING TO DO IN A LITTLE CANOE? THE SEQUESTERING OF SADOMASOCHISM IN WOMEN'S LIVES (1997)

Novick, K.K. (1997). What are you going to do in a little canoe? The sequestering of sadomasochism in women's lives. Unpublished paper presented at the Annual Meeting of Division 39 of APA, Chicago 1997, and the Michigan Psychoanalytic Council 1998. Available on request.

This paper looks at developmental, social, and clinical phenomena, combining perspectives from our understanding of the development of sadomasochistic, closed-system functioning. Our finding that omnipotent beliefs can only persist when validated from the outside is illustrated with discussion of popular children's books and the contribution of culture to gender images that assign sadism to men and masochism to women.

CREATIVITY AND COMPLIANCE: AN INTRODUCTION TO ANNA FREUD'S "THE RELATION OF BEATING PHANTASIES TO A DAYDREAM" (1999)

Novick, K.K. & Novick, J. (1999). Creativity and compliance: An introduction to Anna Freud's, "the relation of beating phantasies to a daydream." In: Female Sexuality: Contemporary Engagements. Ed. Donna Bassin. Northvale, NJ, Jason Aronson, Inc. 1999, 63 – 70.

In this brief introduction we present ideas about specific aspects of closed-system functioning, for instance, the role of the early mother/infant relationship in the development of sadomasochism, and suggest that the act for which the child is beaten is the attempt to be independent and in charge of their own bodies. We assert that masturbation, in boys and girls, often represents to the child an attack on mothers; children may attempt to protect themselves by externalizing responsibility (not using their hands to masturbate) but then still end up being punished.

LOVE IN THE THERAPEUTIC ALLIANCE (2000)

Novick, J. and Novick, K.K. (2000). Love in the therapeutic alliance. JAPA 48: 189 -218

In our two-systems model we distinguish between "objective love" as a central affect of the "open system" and sadomasochistic power relations disguised as love as integral to the "closed system." This paper examines the history of the role of love in treatment and suggests that the two-systems model and the tasks of therapeutic alliance (as objective measures of the open system) provide therapists with a guide through the phases of treatment.

The paper focuses on the therapist's love for the patient and concludes,

"We have also emphasized the ongoing need to distinguish between omnipotent power relations in a closed system of functioning, disguised as love, and the growth-enhancing love that we allocate to open-system functioning. We are suggesting that meaningful and lasting change occurs in the context of the analyst's reality-based respect, admiration and love for the patient."

CULTURAL INTERFERENCES WITH LISTENING TO ADOLESCENTS (2000 [1994])

DeVito, E., Novick, J., and Novick, K.K. (2000). Cultural interferences with listening to adolescents.
J.I.C.A.P. 1:77 -95.

A translation of a paper first published in Italian in 1994. With material from work with Italian and American adolescents we illustrate that the task in adolescence is transformation not separation. This relates to predominantly open-system development.

Two Systems of Self-Regulation (2001)

Novick, J. and Novick, K.K. (2001). Two systems of self-regulation. J. of Psychoanalytic Social Work 8: 95 – 122

Readers who have found this book useful may want to read this article as it is a blue print for this volume. It contains examples of various applications of the two-systems model to technique and theory. In the same issue of this journal you can find an article by Howard Lerner entitled "A Two-Systems approach to the treatment of a disturbed adolescent" which is an early application of the model. This paper has also been helpful to those who have applied the two-systems model to work with parents and those who attempt to integrate the model with the theories of Bion, Klein and Winnicott (Zachrisson 2013).

The Dynamic Application of Research and Evaluation to Theory and Program Development in a Psychoanalytic Preschool Setting (2001)

Novick, K.K., Sorenson, E., Novick, J., and Lerner, H. (2001). The dynamic application of research and evaluation to theory and program development in a psychoanalytic preschool setting. Unpublished paper. Available on request.

This paper describes a research effort over several years to create a psychoanalytic outcome measure for parent education and support and child development in the context of Allen Creek Preschool, a psychoanalytic preschool founded in Ann Arbor, Michigan in 1994. Initial funding was granted by the International Psychoanalytic Association and this paper was presented at the IPA Research Congress in Nice, France in 2002.

The Allen Creek Parenting Scale was a direct application of the two-systems model, in that it described both closed- and open-system functioning in parents in ordinary daily life situations with their children. We were able to track statistically significant changes in parental functioning after only one year in the Allen Creek program.

TRAUMA AND DEFERRED ACTION IN THE REALITY OF ADOLESCENCE (2001)

Novick, J. and Novick, K.K. (2001). Trauma and deferred action in the reality of adolescence. Am. J. Psychoanal. 61:43 – 61

Elaborating on earlier comments regarding Freud's concept of Nachtraglichkeit or Deferred Action we discuss the potential for trauma in adolescence and that trauma can occur by deferred action. We emphasize that adolescence is a time when young people can consolidate open-system or closed-system modes of self-regulation.

RECLAIMING THE LAND (2002)

Novick, K.K. and Novick, J. (2002). Reclaiming the land. Psychoanal. Psychol., 19: 348 – 377.

This is a paper with both a theoretical and what one might call a political agenda, in which we urge psychoanalysts to reclaim aspects of theory and technique that have been ceded to allied fields, cease turning to ever-narrower theories that take the part for the whole, rediscover the clinical utility of application to a broad range of pathologies, and re-establish psychoanalysis as a general psychology with a multi-modal technique. The paper is structured in sections, one for each metapsychological point of view, in which we define its purview, look at applications, relate the issues to findings from other fields, and describe relevant clinical techniques. It can be read as a first exposition of detailed technical ideas that relate to both closed- and open-system issues.

TWO SYSTEMS OF SELF-REGULATION AND THE DIFFERENTIAL APPLICATION OF PSYCHOANALYTIC TECHNIQUE (2003)

Novick, J. and Novick, K.K. (2003). Two systems of self-regulation and the differential application of psychoanalytic technique. American Journal of Psychoanalysis 63: 1-19.

Using clinical material we demonstrate in this paper that the two-systems model allows us to think in terms of two kinds of technique, one that works better to elucidate closed-system functioning, another that enhances open-system functioning. Some clinical techniques can be wasteful or even counterproductive when applied without regard to the context.

THE SUPEREGO AND THE TWO-SYSTEMS MODEL (2004)

Novick, J. and Novick, K.K. (2004). The superego and the two-systems model. Psa. Inq. 24: 232 – 256.

This paper is part of a volume devoted to considering the continuing relevance of the superego concept. We used the lens of the two-systems model to consider a concept that had long been viewed as a cornerstone of psychoanalysis and yet seemed to have been supplanted or ignored by many in the current psychoanalytic discourse. In his introduction to the volume, Wurmser notes that our paper highlights the omnipotence underlying the tyrannical sadism of the closed-system superego and underscores the goal of perfection in the closed system which leads to endless vicious cycles. Lichtenberg, in his summary, states that our open-system developmental perspective is compatible with the intersubjective and self-psychological approaches to normal development and noted that our model "serves as a welcome counterbalance to a limitedly pathologized version of psychic life and a restricted intrapsychic model"(2004, p.329).

A DEVELOPMENTAL THEORY OF SADOMASOCHISM (2005 [2002])

Novick, J. and Novick, K.K. (2005 [2002]). A developmental theory of sadomasochism. Bull. Michigan Psychoanalytic Council; 1: 3 – 27

First published in 2002 in a special issue of the Revue Francaise de Psychanalyse, this English translation not only summarizes our developmental views on sadomasochism but also outlines the applications of the two-systems model to technique, theory, and culture.

WORKING WITH PARENTS MAKES THERAPY WORK (2005)

Novick, K.K. and Novick, J. (2005). Working With Parents Makes Therapy Work. New York: Jason Aronson
Available from Amazon, the publisher, or directly from the authors

The concept of the open system provides theoretical space or permission for analysts to include considerations of interactions with external reality alongside their focus on psychic reality. The most salient external reality for everyone is the family, including siblings, grandparents, extended and blended members, but especially the parents.

We start the book by stating that parents and children are involved in a lifelong complex interaction. The foundational idea from the two system model that everyone has the potential at any point in life to make open- or closed-system choices combined with our intergenerational developmental focus to lay the groundwork for this model of dynamic concurrent parent work. It is an example of how the two-systems model expands the domain.

We posit here that child and adolescent treatment has dual goals. In addition to the classical goal of restoration to the path of progressive development, we add the goal of restoring the parent-child relationship to a life-long positive resource for both. We set the goal for concurrent parent work as movement from closed- to open-system self-regulation for parents as well as child or adolescent patients.

As in this current book, we use the phases of the therapeutic alliance through treatment to help parents become established and consolidated in the phase of parenthood and able then to support and accept positive changes in their children and adolescents.

SOUL BLINDNESS: A CHILD MUST BE SEEN TO BE HEARD (2005)

Novick, J. and Novick, K.K. (2005). Soul Blindness: A child must be seen to be heard. In: Divorce and Custody: Contemporary Developmental Psychoanalytical Perspectives. Ed. L. Gunsberg & P. Hymowitz. Washington, DC: American Psychological Assn. Books. Ch. 7: 81 – 90

Using the cases of a little boy torn between the opposing needs of divorced parents and that of Jessica DeBoer, the adopted child who became the subject of a nationwide controversy as legal and mental health experts took sides in the battle between the adoptive and birth parents over who owned the child, we make use of the concept of "soul blindness" when we talk of such moral dilemmas. We were both very involved in that case as an expert witness and as a consultant. Soul blindness is the inability or refusal to see children as separate people with their own unique feelings, reactions and rights. We suggest that soul blindness is what precedes externalization on to the child, a precondition for abuse and soul murder.

Our ideas about closed-system functioning help elucidate the actions of individuals and institutions involved in such situations.

GOOD GOODBYES: KNOWING HOW TO END IN PSYCHOANALYSIS AND PSYCHOTHERAPY (2006)

Novick, J. and Novick, K.K. (2006). Good Goodbyes: Knowing How to End in Psychoanalysis and Psychotherapy. New York: Aronson (Rowman & Littlefield)
Available from Amazon, the publisher, or directly from the authors

Together and separately we have written many articles about termination of treatment with children, adolescents, and adults. Increasingly our interest in open and closed systems has influenced our work in this area. This book contains both a summary of our work on termination since 1976 and the influence of our newer views. In this book we use the phases of treatment and the therapeutic alliance tasks as organizers. We look at the termination issues from the first phone call to the last goodbye and beyond.

At the end of the book we ask, "What is the relevance of the two systems of self-regulation to termination?" We answer with an exposition of our assumptions, which includes that the goal of treatment can be reformulated as the consolidation of open-system functioning so that the patient has a genuine choice between the two modes of self-regulation and conflict resolution.

EXPANDING THE DOMAIN: PRIVACY, SECRECY, AND CONFIDENTIALITY (2008)

Novick, J. and Novick, K.K. (2008). Expanding the domain: privacy, secrecy and confidentiality. Annual of Psychoanalysis. 2008/2009, 36/37: 145 – 160.

Describing the case of a seriously suicidal adolescent and another of a very talented college student who avoided success, we look at concurrent work with parents of adolescents. We note that the major objection by therapists to concurrent work is the issue of confidentiality. Our two systems developmental model allows us to reframe adolescent tasks and gives us concepts and a language to deal with secrets, dangerous actions, and privacy. We suggest a hierarchy of clinical values with safety in the highest position.

THE RAT MAN AND TWO SYSTEMS OF SELF-REGULATION (2009)

Novick, J. and Novick, K.K. (2009). The Rat Man and two systems of self-regulation. Round Robin Newsletter, APA Division of Psychoanalysis 24, 1: 11-17.

Using Freud's treatment notes and write-up of the case of the "Rat Man" together with contemporary work with a severely obsessional young man, we illustrate that, when we supplement classical techniques with techniques that enhance open-system functioning, as Freud did, we can be more effective in treating OCD.

EMOTIONAL MUSCLE: STRONG PARENTS, STRONG CHILDREN (2010)

Novick, K.K. and Novick, J. Emotional Muscle: Strong Parents, Strong Children.
Indiana: XLibris 2010
Translated into Spanish and Chinese
Available from Amazon, ipbooks, XLibris, or directly from the authors
Website: Buildemotionalmuscle.com

This book, written originally for parents and teachers, is now being used as a textbook for early childhood development in psychoanalytic, psychiatric, and social work trainings. The metaphor of "emotional muscle" is immediately accessible to people of all ages and describes ego functions and general characteristics of the personality that relate largely to open-system functioning. In accessible language, with copious illustrations from ordinary family life, we describe what goes into the development of specific emotional muscles at different stages of development for both parents and children, and why they are important.

Building Emotional Muscle in Children and Parents (2011)

Novick, K.K. & Novick, J. (2011). Building emotional muscle in children and parents. Psychoanal. Study Child, 65: 131-151

Our first published use of the term "emotional muscle" is in our 2001 paper on two systems of self-regulation. The concept arose from clinical work in relation to therapeutic impasse and as a criterion for termination. Emotional muscle is part of the open system and relates to psychoanalytic concepts such as ego strength, frustration tolerance, resilience, positive self-regulation, character, will, protective factors and so forth. We first applied the concept to work in Allen Creek Preschool with great success as summarized in our book for parents and teachers (2010). In this paper we return to the utility of this concept in the clinical sphere as we describe the psychoanalytic provenance and applications of the concept, the support for such a term from other disciplines, and illustrate the clinical use of this metaphor with several cases.

Sex, Drugs, and Rock 'n Roll (2011)

Novick, J. and Novick, K.K. (2011). Sex, drugs and rock and roll: eraan myohais-Nurouusikaisen sadomasokistisen ja avoimen itsesaatelyn muotoja. Nuorisopsykoterapian erityiskysymyksia 13: 57-84.

This paper, currently published in Finnish, illustrates several important dimensions of the interrelationship of the two-systems model with our conceptualization of the therapeutic alliance. The concept of a therapeutic alliance with particular tasks at each phase of treatment links directly with a two-systems model: each task represents an operational definition of open-system goals and development.

One interesting aspect of this case is the long-term impact of prescription drugs for children. This young man had been started on psychotropic and stimulant medication as a preschooler. At 19 when this patient began treatment, he was a heavy marijuana user, abused alcohol, and it wasn't clear whether he still actually used Ritalin and Prozac. He definitely had prescriptions for them, as he sold these drugs in addition to marijuana. In our view, the quick acceptance by doctors, parents and patients of medications with no sound scientific basis represents a wish and closed-system belief in quick, easy omnipotent solutions, rather than a realistic assessment of the work needed to resolve conflicts and find new, open-system realistic ways to regulate the self.

EMOTIONAL MUSCLE FOR THERAPISTS – A STRENGTH-BASED LEARNING MODEL FOR TREATMENT (2012)

Novick, J. and Novick, K.K. (2012). Emotional muscle for therapists – a strength-based learning model for treatment. Bulletin of the Michigan Psychoanalytic Council 8: 3-23

The usefulness of the metaphor of "emotional muscle" was first apparent to us in clinical work. We then applied it to children and parents in other settings, like schools and daycare centers. Our book "Emotional Muscle: Strong Parents, Strong Children" described that applied work with families with children ages birth to 6 years. In this paper we return to clinical applications of emotional muscle, and describe in greater detail techniques derived from the concepts that therapists can use in their clinical work at each phase of treatment. We also suggest that therapists too need to develop emotional muscle as a safeguard against being drawn into closed-system functioning in the therapeutic relationship.

SOME SUGGESTIONS FOR ENGAGING WITH THE CLINICAL PROBLEMS OF MASOCHISM (2012)

Novick, K.K. and Novick, J. Some suggestions for engaging with the clinical problem of masochism. In: The Clinical Problem of Masochism, Eds. D. Holtzman and N. Kulish. Jason Aronson/Rowman and Littlefield: Lanham, MD. 2012, pp. 51-75.

Closed-system functioning, with its omnipotent core beliefs, is the major obstacle in the transition from late adolescence to adulthood. Each of the sadomasochistic strands from earlier levels can be intensified under the impact of the real changes of adolescence. In this chapter we describe treatment of a late adolescent in order to highlight several core points in our two-systems model.

One is that we have found that sadism and masochism are always connected; the bridge is the formation of magical omnipotent beliefs as a major defense against helplessness. Anna Freud elaborated on the idea that fear of helplessness underlies all the other anxieties in the classical sequence. We, along with Freud and all other subsequent developmental psychologists, see mastery as a fundamental human need. The opposite of mastery is helplessness in relation to inner and outer forces. But we differentiate between closed, omnipotent, sadomasochistic modes of mastery and open, competent methods.

The fact that the aim of self-regulation is the same in both systems creates a point of entry for work on the open- and closed-system alternative ways to meet basic needs.

ALTRUISTIC ANALYSIS (2012)

Novick, J. & Novick, K.K. (2012). Altruistic analysis. In: The Anna Freud Tradition. Ed. Norka Malberg and Joan Raphael-Leff. London, Karnac Books Ltd. Ch.31, 365 – 368

Through the history of child analysis, Anna Freud and her colleagues made service to the community and application of psychoanalytic ideas to a range of child and family programs central to the identity of child analysts. We note that none of these activities were done for riches, academic advancement, research grants or professional status – so we called this "altruistic analysis." The capacity to act beyond one's own immediate needs, to serve others, is to us an important element of open-system functioning and an indispensable definer of achieving the phase of parenthood. Thus we include this paper here as an example of ways in which the two-systems model applies also to analysts and our activities as a group.

TWO SYSTEMS AND DEFENSES (2013)

Novick, J., Novick, K.K. (2013). Two Systems and Defenses. Psychoanal. Rev. 100:185-200.

In this paper we suggest that Freud's concept of defense differentiated psychoanalysis from other medical and psychological theories of personality development and functioning then and now. Reclaiming the concept's centrality and linking it with interdisciplinary research findings, we illustrate our extension of defense into a two-system model of self-protection and self-regulation with a clinical example. We suggest that the two-system model allows for the reintegration of defense into a multidimensional psychoanalytic theory and multimodal therapeutic technique. We suggest that the alternative to unconscious defenses which operate in closed-system functioning, is emotional muscle, capacities that provide safety by supporting and nurturing open-system functioning and groundedness in reality.

DISCUSSION OF THE CASE OF DIANE (2013)

Novick, J. and Novick, K.K. Discussion of the case of Diane. In: Battling the Life and Death Forces of Sadomasochism: Clinical Perspectives. Eds: H. Basseches, P. Ellman, N. Goodman. Karnac: London. 2013, pp. 63-78.

This case discussion highlights the role of pain in sadomasochistic functioning and relationships, including the therapeutic interaction. The experience of pain in the body and the mind throughout development and how it is used to perpetuate closed-system solutions is vivid in this patient's treatment, as is the poignant counterpoint with open-system moments. We focus also on the counter-reactive and countertransferential aspects of closed-system relationships in treatment and underscore technical approaches to them.

AN ANNA FREUDIAN COMMENTARY
ON MRS. H (2013)

Novick, J. and Novick, K.K. An Anna Freudian commentary on Mrs. H. In: Psychotherapy in the Wake of War. Ed. B. Huppertz. Jason Aronson/Rowman and Littlefield, Lanham, MD. 2013, pp. 159-166.

In this case discussion, we anchor our two system model in a larger psychoanalytic tradition, stating that we think it is "the richness, complexity, and integrative power of the metapsychological theory that remains the solid ground on which all other ideas can build." Central to our developmental point of view is our extension of Anna Freud's concept of progressive development to a growth principle that is rooted in perennial psychoanalytic ideas like the autonomous ego instincts, the dual-track model of development, life-cycle epigenesis, and more (Freud 1915, Hartman 1939, Erikson 1950, White 1959, Lichtenberg 1989, Grotstein 1986, 1994, Young-Bruehl 2009). We apply these ideas to the case in point, noting that we look from the beginning at the whole person, trying to understand whether and why lifelong growth has stalled. Rather than using a nosological medical model that tabulates symptoms to arrive at a diagnosis, we listen for any vicious cycles of static self-destructive functioning. But we also listen for strengths, and the presence of open-system ego capacities, even those that have been coopted to the service of closed-system sadomasochistic functioning.

PSYCHOANALYSIS AND CHILD REARING (2014)

Novick, K.K. and Novick, J. (2014). Psychoanalysis and child rearing. Psa. Inquiry 34: 440 – 451.

This paper is a contribution to a volume on "Specialness, Grandiosity, Omnipotence, Entitlement and Indulgence: Changing Theories of Narcissism, Attitudes, and Culture." In this paper we suggest that current controversies around the psychoanalytic concepts of narcissism, omnipotence, specialness and so forth derive from reliance on a single-track developmental model. A single-track model, used implicitly or explicitly by almost all psychoanalytic theorists, posits that normal infants and children function in ways that would be considered pathological in later life. This way of thinking is contradicted by modern infant and developmental research. Additionally, it contradicts common-sense experience and is therefore not a useful model for parenting.

On the other hand, Freud and many other writers also posited a dual-track model, which simultaneously allows for both healthy and pathological choices throughout life. In this paper, we describe the history of psychoanalytic influence on cultural ideas of child rearing and suggest some of the ways in which a dual-track model, which we have elaborated as "two systems of self-regulation," can be usefully applied to theory, technique, and applications with all those involved with children.

GREEN WOUNDS: REVENGE AS PRESERVER OF THE SELF (2014)

Novick, K.K. Green wounds: revenge as preserver of the self. In: S. Akhtar and H. Parens, Eds., Revenge: Narcissistic Injury, Rage, and Retaliation. 2014, Jason Aronson/Rowman and Littlefield, Lanham MD. pp.19-31.

This clinical paper describes the role of revenge in keeping a self-representation intact under the assault of intergenerational pathology and intense internal and interpersonal conflicts. The two-systems model was helpful in conceptualizing this child's history and experience in terms of his active choice of a closed-system vengeful path in early childhood when no other solutions to his helplessness seemed available to him. Rather dramatic reality interventions underscored the importance of staying mindful of open-system aspects.

WORKING WITH "OUT-OF-CONTROL" CHILDREN – A TWO-SYSTEMS APPROACH (2015)

Novick, J. and Novick, K.K. (2015). Working with "out-of-control" children – a two-systems approach. Psychoanalytic Study of the Child 69: 153-188.

In this paper we apply a two-systems approach to demonstrate improved treatment possibilities and outcomes in this group of children, and suggest that psychoanalysis can be defined as a multi-modal strengths-based learning experience. Using clinical material from the analysis of an aggressive, "out-of-control" child, we discuss how these behaviors and symptoms are better understood as an actively constructed closed-system effort at self-regulation than as a deficiency in capacity or primitive, lagging development. Simultaneous work on open-system strengths is crucial to promoting change and the gradual development of positive alternatives. We illustrate how a two-systems framework can allow for an expanded repertoire of techniques and reclaim some psychoanalytic concepts that have fallen into disuse.

MORALITY IN THE MODERN WORLD (2015)

Novick, J. and Novick, K.K. (2016 in press). Morality in the modern world.

This paper builds on our earlier formulations of closed- and open-system superego functioning. Here we make the point that, even if psychoanalytic theorists have largely moved away from consideration of the superego, there is still a need for a conceptualization of the psychic representation of self-regulation.

Here we apply our epigenetic two-systems model to moral development – the conscience component of self-regulation – with material from several different cases where we trace derivatives and elements from different developmental phases as they appeared in their adult functioning. This paper includes discussion of the appeal to young people looking for quick, closed-system solutions to powerlessness as provided by demagogues and radical movements.

A Two-systems Approach to OCD (2016)

Novick, J. and Novick, K.K. (2016 in press). A two-systems approach to OCD.

Long considered an ailment for which psychoanalysis was the treatment of choice, it is now quite rare for obsessional patients to be referred for psychotherapy or analysis, even by analysts. In this paper we suggest that a broadened theoretical and technical understanding, based on the two-systems model, can revive the relevance of psychodynamic thinking and treatment for OCD.

Building on our thinking in relation to Freud's case of the Rat Man (Novick and Novick 2009), here we describe work with a young man in which the initial approach was to say that his OCD seemed to be a circular way of thinking that he had used to protect himself for many years. It wasn't yet clear what he was protecting himself from. The first part of any work would be to figure that out so that he could explore alternative solutions that wouldn't be so costly in his life. That wouldn't mean that his old OCD protections would be taken away. He would always have those. The goal of a treatment would be to generate more options.

The paper details techniques designed to address both open- and closed-system functioning. We think that this illustrates the continuing relevance of psychoanalysis to the treatment of OCD and the utility of applying a two-systems approach, with its capacity to reclaim and include a broad range of psychoanalytic techniques.

Some Suggested Distinguishables Generated by a Two-Systems Model

We have found that the two-systems model can highlight important differences between various psychoanalytic concepts. We offer an illustrative list below with the idea that people will think about how to distinguish between these manifestations and consider further possibilities.

CLOSED-SYSTEM AND OPEN-SYSTEM ALTERNATIVES:

Envy	Admiration
Guilt/Regret	Shame/Remorse
Omnipotence	Competence
Enthrallment	Love
Authoritarian	Authoritative
Repetition	Transformation
Addictive High	Creative Joy
Control of Other	Mutual Enhancement
Defense	Emotional Muscle
Dependency	Interdependence
Secrecy	Privacy
Aggression	Assertion
Separation	Separateness
States	Signals
Delusion	Illusion
Belief	Wish/Daydream/Fantasy
False Self	True Self
Perfection	Aspiration/Good Enough
Depression	Sadness
Coercion	Collaboration
Revenge	Reparation/Reconciliation
Soul Blindness	Empathy
Guilt/Blame	Responsibility/Usable Concern
Myth	Realistic Reconstruction
Triumph	Satisfaction
Despair	Hope

References

Balint, M. (1968). The Basic Fault. London: Tavistock

Barrett, T.F. (2008). Manic Defenses against Loneliness in Adolescence. Psychoanal. St. Child 63:111-136

Bergmann, M. (1988). On the fate of the intrapsychic image of the psychoanalyst after termination of the analysis. Psychoanal. Study Child 43: 137-154.

——— (1997). Termination: the Achilles heel of psychoanalytic technique. Psychoanal. Psych. 14: 163-174.

Botella, C. and Botella, S. (2005). The Work of Psychic Figurability: Mental States Without Representation. Hove, England and New York: Brunner-Routledge.

Bowlby, J. (1969), Attachment and Loss, Vol. 1 Attachment, New York, Hogarth Press.

——— (1973), Attachment and Loss, Vol. 2 Separation: Anxiety and Anger, New York, Basic Books.

——— (1980), Attachment and Loss, Vol. 3 Sadness and Depression, London, Hogarth Press.

Britton, R. (2010). There is no end of the line: terminating the interminable. In: Good Enough Endings: Breaks, Interruptions, and Terminations From Contemporary Relational Perspectives, Ed. Jill Salberg. New York: Routledge. pp. 39-50.

Burger, K., Stice, E., and Yokum, S. (2013). Relative ability of fat and sugar tastes to activate reward, gustatory, and somatosensory regions. The American Journal of Clinical Nutrition, 98(6), 1377-84.

Cicchetti, D. and Rogosch, F. (1996). Equifinality and multifinality in developmental psychopathology. Development and Psychopathology 8: 597-600.

Colarusso, C.A. and Nemiroff, R.A. (1979). Some observations and hypotheses about the psychoanalytic theory of adult development. American Journal of Psycho-analysis 60: 59.

——— (1981). Adult Development: A New Dimension in Psychodynamic Theory and Practice. Plenum Press: New York.

Colarusso, C. and Montero, G. J. (2007). Transience during midlife as an adult psychic organizer: the midlife transition and crisis continuum. Psychoanalytic Study of the Child 62: 329 – 358.

DeVito, E., Novick, J., and Novick, K.K. (2000). Cultural interferences with listening to adolescents. *J.I.C.A.P.* 1: 77-95.

Doidge, N. (2007). The Brain That Changes Itself. Penguin Books, London.

Emde, R. (1988), Development terminable and interminable. 1. Innate and motivational factors from infancy, *Int. J. Psycho-Anal.*, 69, 23-42.

Erikson, E. (1950). Childhood and Society. New York: Norton

Feldman, S. and Zaller, J. (1992). "A Simple Theory of the Survey Response: Answering Questions vs. Revealing Preferences," *American Journal of Political Science*, August 1992.

Freud, A. (1965), Normality and Pathology in Childhood, *Writings*, 6, 3-273, New York, International Universities Press.

Freud, S. (1895). Studies in hysteria, S.E. 2, 3-335.

——— (1900). The interpretation of dreams. S. E. 4

——— (1905). Three essays on the theory of sexuality. S.E. 7:125-243.

——— (1909). Notes upon a case of obsessional neurosis. S.E. 10: 153-320

—— (1913), On beginning the treatment (Further recommendations on the technique of psycho-analysis I), S.E. 12, 123-144.

—— (1915), Instincts and their vicissitudes, S.E.14, 117-140.

—— (1919), A child is being beaten, S.E.17, 175-204.

—— (1920), Beyond the pleasure principle, S.E. 18, 3-64.

—— (1940 [1938]), An outline of psychoanalysis, S.E. 23, 141-207.

Furman, E. (1992). Toddlers and Their Mothers. New Haven, CT. Yale University Press.

—— (1985), On fusion, integration, and feeling good. *Psychoanal. St. Child*, 40:81-110.

Furman, R.A. and Furman, E. (1984). Intermittent decathexis: a type of parental dysfunction. Int. J. Psycho-Anal., 65: 423-433.

Giedd, J., Lalonde, F., Celano, M., White , S., Wallace, G., Lee, N., and Lenroot, R. (2009). Anatomical brain magnetic resonance imaging of typically developing children and adolescents. J. Am. Acad. Child Adolesc. Psychiatry, 48:5, 465-470.

Glover, E. (1955). The Technique of Psychoanalysis. New York: International Universities Press.

Greenson, R. (1965) The working alliance and the transference neurosis. In Explorations in Psychoanalysis, pp. 199-224. New York: International Universities Press, 1978.

—— (1971). The "real" relationship between the patient and the psychoanalyst. In Explorations in Psychoanalysis, pp. 425-440. New York: International University Press, 1978.

Grotstein, J. (1986), The psychology of powerlessness: disorders of self-regulation and interactional regulation as a newer paradigm for psychopathology, *Psych. Inquiry*, 6, 93-118.

—— (1994), Foreword to Allan N. Shore Affect Regulation and the Origin of the Self,

Hillsdale, NJ, Lawrence Erlbaum Associates, pp. xxi-xxviii.

Hartmann, H. (1939). Ego Psychology and the Problem of Adaptation, New York, International Universities Press (1958).

Homann, E. (2013). Development of a Rorschach scale of Omnipotence and its Relation to Closed-System Information Processing. Unpublished Research, Eastern Michigan University.

Horney K. (1939). New Ways in Psychoanalysis. New York: Norton.

Hughes, C.H. (1884). Borderland psychiatric records: prodromal symptoms of psychical impairment. Alienist and Neurologist 5: 85-91.

Jacques, E. (1965). Death and the midlife crisis. Int. J. Psychoanal. 46: 502-514.

Kantrowitz, J. (1997). The Patient's Impact on the Analyst. New York: The Analytic Press.

Laufer, M. and Laufer, M.E. (1984). Adolescence and Developmental Breakdown. New Haven: Yale University Press.

Levine, H.B., Reed, G. and Scarfone, D., eds. (2013). Unrepresented States And The Construction Of Meaning: Clinical And Theoretical Contributions. London: Karnac.

Lichtenberg, J. (1989). Psychoanalysis and Motivation. Hillsdale, NJ: Analytic Press

Lichtenberg, L., Lachmann, F., and Fosshage, J. (1992), Self and Motivational Systems: Toward A Theory of Technique. Hillsdale, NJ, Analytic Press.

——— (1996). The Clinical Exchange: Techniques Derived from Self and Motivational Systems. Hillsdale, NJ: Analytic Press.

Loewenstein, R.M. (1969). Developments in the theory of transference in the last fifty years. Int. J. Psycho-Anal. 50: 583-588.

Mayr, E. (1988). Toward a New Philosophy of Biology. Cambridge, MA: Harvard University Press.

National Research Council and Institute of Medicine (2000). From Neurons to Neighborhoods: The Science of Early Development. Jack P. Shonkoff and Deborah A. Phillips, Eds. Washington, D.C.: National Academy Press.

Novick, J., (1976). The termination of treatment of an adolescent boy. J. Child Psychotherapy 4:5-28.

——— (1980). Negative therapeutic motivation and negative therapeutic alliance. Psychoanal. Study Child 35: 299 -319.

——— (1982). Varieties of transference in the analysis of an adolescent. Int. J. Psycho-Anal. 63:139-148.

——— (1982). Termination: Themes and issues. Psychoanalytic Inquiry 2:329-365.

——— (1988). Timing of termination. Int. Rev. Psycho-Anal. 69: 307-318.

——— (1990). Comments on termination in child, adolescent, and adult analysis. Psychoanal. Study Child 45: 419-436.

——— (1992). The therapeutic alliance, a concept revisited. Child Analysis 3: 90- 100.

——— (1997). Termination conceivable and inconceivable. Psychoanalytic Psychology 14: 145-162.

——— (1999). Deferred action and recovered memory: the organization of memory in the reality of adolescence. Child Analysis 10: 65-93.

Novick, J. and Kelly, K. (1970). Projection and Externalization. Psychoanalytic Study of the Child 25: 69-95.

Novick, J. and Novick, K.K. (1972). Beating Fantasies in Children. Int. J. Psycho-Anal. 53:237-242.

——— (1991). Some Comments on Masochism and the Delusion of Omnipotence from a Developmental Perspective. JAPA, vol. 39, 2:307-331.

——— (1996a). A developmental perspective on omnipotence. J. Clinical Psychoanalysis. 5: 124-173.

——— (1996b). Fearful Symmetry: The Development and Treatment of Sadomasochism. Northvale, NJ: Jason Aronson.

——— (1999), Dialogue on violence, terror and persecution: response to W. Sofsky, *International Psychoanalysis, Newsletter of the IPA*, 8, 35-37.

——— (2000). Love in the therapeutic alliance. JAPA 48: 189-218.

——— (2001). Trauma and deferred action in the reality of adolescence. American Journal of Psychoanalysis, 61, 43-61.

——— (2004). The superego and the two-system model. Psychoanalytic Inquiry 24 (2), 232-356.

———Good Goodbyes: Knowing How To End in Psychoanalysis and Psychotherapy. New York: Aronson (Rowman and Littlefield) 2006

——— (2008). Expanding the domain: privacy, secrecy and confidentiality. Annual of Psychoanalysis 2008-2009, 36/37: 145-160.

——— (2009). The Rat Man and two systems of self-regulation. Round Robin Newsletter, APA Division of Psychoanalysis 24, 1:1, 11-17.

——— (2012). Emotional muscle in therapists – a strengths-based learning model for treatment. Bull. Michigan Psychoanalytic Council 8: 3-23.

——— (2012). Review of Good Enough Endings: Breaks, Interruptions, and Termination from a Contemporary Relational Perspective. Edited by Jill Salberg. New York: Routledge, 2010 Psychoanalytic Quarterly 81: 474-480

——— (2013). Two Systems and Defenses. Psychoanal. Rev. 100:185-200.

——— (2015). Working with "out-of-control" children – a two-systems approach. Psychoanalytic Study of the Child 69: 153-188.

Novick, K.K. and Novick, J. (1987). The essence of masochism. Psychoanalytic Study of the Child 42:353-384.

——— (1994). Post-oedipal transformations: latency, adolescence and pathogenesis. Journal of the American Psychoanalytic Association 42:143-170

——— (1998). An application of the concept of the therapeutic alliance to sadomasochistic pathology. Journal of the American Psychoanalytic Association 46: 813-846.

——— (1999), Creativity and Compliance: An introduction to Anna Freud's "The relation of beating fantasies to day dream," in ed., Donna Bassin, Female Sexuality: Contemporary Engagements, Northvale, NJ, Jason Aronson, 1999, pp.63-70.

——— (2002). Reclaiming the land. Psychoanalytic Psychology 19: 2, 348-377.

——— (2003). Two systems of self-regulation and the differential application of psychoanalytic technique. American Journal of Psychoanalysis 63: 1-19.

——— (2010). Emotional Muscle: Strong Parents, Strong Children. XLibris: Indiana

——— (2011). Building Emotional Muscle in Children and Parents. Psychoanal. St. Child, 65:131-151.

Orgel, S. (1974), Fusion with the victim and suicide. *Int. J. Psycho-Anal.*, 55:532-538

Rathbone, J. (2001). Anatomy of Masochism. New York: Klewer Academic/Plenum Publishers.

Russell, I. (1884). The borderlands of insanity. Alienist and Neurologist 5: 457-471.

Salberg, J., Ed. (2010). Good Enough Endings: Breaks, Interruptions, and Terminations From Contemporary Relational Perspectives. New York: Routledge.

Steiner, J. (1993). Psychic Retreats. London: Routledge.

Stern, D.W. (1985). The Interpersonal World of the Infant. New York: Basic Books.

Sugarman, A. (2015). Monday-morning quarterbacking: a senior analyst uses his early work to discuss contemporary child and adolescent psychoanalytic technique. Psychoanal. Study Child 69: 189-215.

Tustin, F. (1994). The perpetuation of an error. J. Ch. Psychotherapy 20, 3-23.

Viorst, J. (1982). Experiences of loss at end of analysis: the analyst's response to termination. Psychoanalytic Inquiry 2: 399-418.

von Bertalanffy, L. (1968). General Systems Theory. New York: Braziller.

Weiss, J. (1993). How Psychotherapy Works: Process and Technique. New York: Guilford Press.

——— (1998), Bondage fantasies and beating fantasies. Psychoanal. Q. 67, 626-644.

White, R.W. (1959), Motivation reconsidered: the concept of competence. Psychological Review 66, 5, 297-333.

Winnicott, D.W. (1949), The ordinary devoted mother and her baby, in The Child, the Family, and the Outside World. Middlesex, England, Penguin Books, 1964, pp.15-18.

——— (1960). Ego distortion in terms of true and false self. In: The Maturational Processes and the Facilitating Environment. London: Hogarth Press. pp.140-152.

——— (1988). Human Nature. New York: Brunner/Mazel.

Wurmser, L. (1994). A time of questioning: the severely disturbed patient within classical analysis. The Annual of Psychoanalysis, Ed. J.A. Winer, 22, 173-207. Chicago: Chicago Institute of Psychoanalysis.

——— (1996). Trauma, inner conflict, and the vicious cycles of repetition. Scandinavian Psychoanalytic Review, 19, 17-45.

Young-Bruehl, E. (2009). Childism – Prejudice Against Children. Contemporary Psychoanal. 45: 251-265.

Zachrisson, A. (2013). The internal/external issue. Psychoanal.Study Child. 67:249-274

Zetzel, E.R. (1965). The theory of therapy in relation to a developmental model of the psychic apparatus. Int. J. Psycho-Anal. 46:39-52.

About the Authors

Jack Novick, M.A., Ph.D, and Kerry Kelly Novick are child, adolescent and adult psychoanalysts. Training and Supervising Analysts of the International Psychoanalytic Association, they serve on the faculties of numerous training centers in the United States. They first trained with Anna Freud in London, England and, in addition to their clinical work over the past 50 years, have been active in teaching, research, professional organizations and the community. They joined with other colleagues to found the award-winning non-profit Allen Creek Preschool in Ann Arbor, Michigan and the international Alliance For Psychoanalytic Schools.

Both Jack and Kerry have served as Chairs of the Child and Adolescent Analysis Committee at the Michigan Psychoanalytic Institute, and were instrumental in starting the first integrated child and adult training curriculum.

Kerry has been elected a Councilor-at-Large on the Board of the American Psychoanalytic Association, is a past President of the Association for Child Psychoanalysis, and is Chair of the Child and Adolescent Psychoanalysis Committee of the International Psychoanalytic Association.

Jack served two terms as North American Representative on the Board of the International Psychoanalytic Association, and is President-Elect of the Association for Child Psychoanalysis.

Jack and Kerry Novick have written extensively since the 1960s, with many book chapters and over 100 articles published in major professional journals. Their book « Fearful Symmetry : The Development and Treatment of Sadomasochism » appeared in 1996 and was re-issued in paperback in 2007. « Working With Parents Makes Therapy Work » appeared in 2005, and « Good Goodbyes : Knowing How To End In Psychotherapy and Psychoanalysis » was published in 2006. « Emotional Muscle : Strong Parents, Strong Children » appeared in 2010. All their books have been translated into several other languages and are used in training mental health professionals around the world.

They have both held academic and research positions and are currently in private practice.

Praise for their earlier books

On Fearful Symmetry

They give us a landmark work. This book will prove indispensable to mental health professionals.
Leonard Shengold, M.D.

Their clarity of thought and clinical focus makes their book a joy to read.
Robert L. Tyson, M.D., F.R.C. Psych.

The book offers an illuminating, rich, and rewarding study of the enigmatic attachment or addiction to pain, and to pleasure in pain.
Harold P. Blum, M.D.

On Working With Parents Makes Therapy Work

This is an extraordinarily important contribution. Their work underscores the inevitable ongoing interaction between parent functioning and child development.

Leon Hoffman, M.D.

This book offers further elaboration and new applications of the Novicks' earlier research on the two-systems model. It is so well-written ... it represents a bold new vision of the role of parents in the psychoanalytic treatment of child and adolescent patients.

Jerrold R. Brandell, MSSW, Ph.D.

On Good Goodbyes

Through vivid and compelling vignettes ... they demonstrate that ... a patient's system of self-regulation can be transformed from one that is joyless, constricted and closed to one that is healthy, alive and open.

William B. Meyer, MSW, BCD

On Emotional Muscle

The authors' expertise with living, breathing children comes through on every page.

Diane Manning, Ph.D.

A must-read for anyone committed to understanding how values are conveyed and how the development of character can be supported.

Michelle Graves, M.A.

Emotional Muscle is a book that is needed, relevant, and should be required reading for all parents and educators.

Kathleen Kryza, M.A.

In this book ... they do for these early years what Erik Erikson did on the broader canvas of the human life cycle in his classic Childhood and Society...Their book will be a valuable resource to generations of parents, daycare workers, preschool teachers and others caring for young children.

Paul Brinich, Ph.D.

Notes

[1] Freud 1919, p.189

[2] J. Novick and K.K. Novick 1972

[3] K.K. Novick and J. Novick 1987; J. Novick and K.K. Novick 1996

[4] ibid 1987

[5] National Research Council, Shonkoff and Phillips 2000, p.3

[6] Freud 1913, p.183

[7] "Perversion" is a term borrowed originally from theology, where it denotes a deviation from the path of true doctrine. 19th-century sexologists, including Freud, used it to describe extreme variations from what they considered mature genital sexuality. Our usage builds on these to bring in distortions of power relationships that adversely affect functioning over time, and relates specifically to interferences in the path of progressive development springing from symptoms or character pathology.

[8] Freud 1895, 1913, 1920, 1940[1938] explicitly delineated an "original reality ego" (1915, p.136) that preceded the "purified pleasure ego" (ibid., p.136). He was followed notably by Hartman 1939, Horney 1939, Erikson 1950, Anna Freud 1965, Bowlby 1969, 1973, 1980, White 1959, and Winnicott 1949. Some current analysts are also working within this dual-track tradition, such as Lichtenberg and his colleagues 1989, 1992, 1996, Grotstein 1986, 1994, and Emde 1988.

[9] Cicchetti and Rogosch 1996; Mayr 1988 and von Bertalanffy 1968.

[10] J. Novick and K.K. Novick, 1991, 1996a, 1996b; K.K. Novick and J. Novick, 1998

[11] Freud 1900.

[12] Freud's *nachtraglichkeit* – see K.K. Novick and J. Novick 1994; J. Novick 1999, 2001a

[13] K.K. Novick and J. Novick 2010, 2011, 2012

[14] J. Novick and K.K. Novick 1972, 1991, 1996a, 1996b, 2000; K.K. Novick and J. Novick 1987, 1998

[15] J. Novick and K.K. Novick 1991, 2000, 2001; J. Weiss 1993, 1998

[16] Novick & Novick 1994, 2001a; J. Novick 1999

[17] K.K. Novick and J. Novick 1994

[18] ibid

[19] Piontelli 1992; Fonagy, Steele, Moran, Steele, and Higgitt 1993

[20] A. Freud 1970 [1966]

[21] We have chosen to use "I" when referring to the analyst in actual clinical interactions, and the collective "we/our/us" when describing our joint, general theoretical, technical and clinical formulations. The "I" is an attempt to capture some of the immediacy of the work and it also adds another layer of confidentiality to the reported clinical material.

[22] Botella and Botella 2005; Levine, Reed, and Scarfone 2013.

[23] From 1982 to 1992, we were part of a research program, with Drs. Donald Silver and B. Kay Campbell, studying the development of relationships between adolescent mothers rejected by their families and their babies. We followed eighty-five pairs through their two-year stay in a residential center, which provided schooling, therapy, medical and social supports for the mothers, and medical and day-care services for the babies. Research data included periodic videotaping as a developmental record, therapy notes, cottage observations, medical and social history records, and case information discussions. In the videotapes of adolescent mothers feeding, bathing, or playing with their babies we may track the development of dysphoric interactions between parent and child that become a source of pain the baby learns to control in the effort to defend against helplessness.

[24] Stern 1985, p. 255.

[25] E. Furman 1985; Orgel 1974

[26] J. Novick and K.K. Novick 2013

[27] At various points in this book, we refer to interactions between a child and a "mother." Sometimes that makes literal sense, as many interactions are specific to a female parent and a baby. Sometimes, however, we have used "mother" and "parent" interchangeably, to denote the early important people in a child's life.

[28] Adapted from J. Novick and K.K. Novick 1996

[29] Adapted from above paper.

[30] K.K. Novick and J. Novick 2010

[31] ibid

[32] Adapted from K.K. Novick and J. Novick 2010

[33] K.K. Novick and J. Novick 1987

[34] J. Novick and K.K. Novick 1991

[35] K.K. Novick and J. Novick 1994.

[36] Because adolescent development is so complex, each step takes time, different amounts of time for each person. Hence the dangers of premature closure at any point along the way. Pressure on young people grappling with body dysphoria or body dysmorphic issues to make irrevocable choices exemplifies the difficulty. Social pressure on teens to declare sexual orientation before they are sure can have serious effects. Support for the emotional muscles involved with tolerating ambiguity, uncertainty and waiting may be crucial for helping adolescents negotiate these arenas of their growth.

[37] In an endnote to the introduction we began to address our usage of the terms "perverse" and "perversion." These words have been used by many in ways that imply negative value judgments and probably reflect prevailing cultural ideas of normality and pathology at the time of the discussion. As we noted earlier, we have adopted Anna Freud's criterion of "restoration to the path of progressive development" in a general way as a goal of treatment and a measure of change. But it begs the question simply to substitute one word for another. We will discuss this more fully in the later chapters on technique in treatment, but note here that we operationalize Anna Freud's idea as a cost/benefit assessment, with a sense that this is a more neutral and objective way to talk about charged issues. What does a person get from a particular behavior or practice? What functions does it serve or needs does it meet? What does that cost in terms of impact on other aspects of life and experience?

[38] Erikson 1950

[39] Colarusso and Nemiroff are among the few psychoanalysts who have looked at development through adulthood. See, for instance 1979 and 1981.

[40] Giedd 2009

[41] Laufer and Laufer 1984

[42] T. Barrett 2008

[43] Devito, Novick, and Novick 1994, 2000.

[44] The non-profit international Alliance for Psychoanalytic Schools promotes the collaborative work of educators and psychoanalysts in many different settings. For further information, please see the APS website at psychoanalyticschools.org.

[45] E. Furman 1992.

[46] Confirmation of this link comes from political science and social science studies, where the most reliable measure of the personality trait of potential authoritarianism can be discerned from answers to questions about parenting goals. We reproduce them here because of their importance.
Feldman and Zaller 1992.

>   1.   Please tell me which one you think is more important for a child to have: independence or respect for elders?
>
>   2.   Please tell me which one you think is more important for a child to have: obedience or self-reliance?
>
>   3.   Please tell me which one you think is more important for a child to have: to be considerate or to be well-behaved?
>
>   4.   Please tell me which one you think is more important for a child to have: curiosity or good manners?

[47] Colarusso and Montero 2007

[48] Erikson 1950

[49] Jacques 1965

[50] Freud 1895

[51] Glover 1955

[52] Freud 1905; A. Freud 1965

[53] Erikson 1950, pp.219-234

[54] Zetzel 1965

[55] J. Novick and K.K. Novick 1991, 1996

[56] J. Novick and K.K. Novick 2012; K.K. Novick and J. Novick 2010, 2011

[57] Freud 1895

[58] Greenson 1965, 1971

[59] Balint, M. 1968

[60] J. Novick 1976, 1982a, 1982b, 1988, 1990, 1992, 1997; K.K. Novick and J. Novick 1991, 1996

[61] K.K. Novick and J. Novick 1987, 1991, 1992, 1996

[62] J. Novick 1992, J. Novick and K.K. Novick 1996

[63] K.K. Novick and J. Novick 1998

[64] Winnicott 1988

[65] K.K. Novick and J. Novick 2003

[66] K.K. Novick and J. Novick 2002

[67] Hughes 1884; Russell 1884

[68] J. Novick and K.K. Novick 2005, 2012

[69] In this book we are generally using clinical examples from work with adults, but we make a similar request in relation to child and adolescent patients, when we ask parents to fill out a short developmental history form to return before we meet. More description and discussion, and a sample form, may be found in our book "Working With Parents Makes Therapy Work" (2005).

[70] Working arrangements:

1. Clients are responsible for payment for all scheduled sessions, unless there is 30 day's notice. We will try to reschedule missed sessions to the extent possible.

2. Payment is due at the beginning of the last session of the month.

3. No significant changes in treatment structure or arrangements (for example, frequency, fees, ending) will be made without 1 month's (4 working weeks) notice from therapist or client.

4. Anonymous, disguised material may be used for teaching or research purposes.

[71] In this chapter we have chosen to use "I" when referring to the analyst in actual clinical interactions, and the collective "we/our/us" when describing our joint, general theoretical, technical and clinical formulations. The "I" is an attempt to capture some of the immediacy of the work and it also adds another layer of confidentiality to the reported clinical material.

[72] Adapted from J. Novick and K.K. Novick 1996b, pp.87, 363

[73] A major two-systems differentiation is between open-system "objective love" and closed-system enthrallment. Building on the work of Freud, Winnicott and Loewald we trace the gradual development of mutual respect, admiration, and objective love between patient and therapist through the phases of treatment. For a detailed description of examples of this evolution in the treatment relationship, please see our paper "Love in the Therapeutic Alliance" (2000).

[74] Adapted from K.K. Novick and J. Novick 1998

[75] J. Novick and K.K. Novick 2000

[76] J. Novick and K.K. Novick 1996b, 2000, 2002; K.K. Novick and J. Novick 1998

[77] K.K. Novick and J. Novick, 1998, p. 816

[78] We differentiate between privacy, a given of mental life in humans that rests on respect for oneself and others as separate individuals, and secrecy, a motivated withholding that is often hostile and is used to control or avoid genuine contact with others. Confidentiality should be maintained in support of privacy and not for the sake of secrecy. Detailed discussion can be found in our paper "Expanding the Domain" (2008), and in our book "Working With Parents Makes Therapy Work" (2005).

[79] J. Novick 1980; J. Novick and K.K. Novick, 1996b

[80] For more discussion of this difference, please see the note on narcissism in our earlier chapter on infancy.

[81] J. Novick and K.K. Novick 1994, 2005; Wurmser 1994, 1996

[82] Steiner 1993

[83] J. Novick and K.K. Novick 1996a

[84] Winnicott 1960

[85] For more detailed description and discussion of anxieties, defenses and reactions in significant others and in parents, see tables and text in our parent work book, K.K. Novick and J. Novick 2005. See also J. Novick and K.K. Novick 2015.

[86] J. Novick and K.K. Novick 2005

[87] K.K. Novick and J. Novick 2010, 2011.

[88] J. Novick and K.K. Novick 2004.

[89] Psychoanalytic ideas go in and out of fashion for various reasons. We suggest that reconstruction may have fallen out of favor because it was sometimes misused in a closed-system, authoritarian way. Analysts sometimes either *told* patients what happened in their pasts or developed images of implausible one-to-one correspondence with theorized infantile experience. We see an alternative in what we call "open-system reconstruction," where patient and analyst are developing a life narrative that makes sense to them both in the context of everything they know and experience. It has to be consistent with real

knowledge from developmental research and child observation, as well as shared understanding of the complexity for the patient of her experience with her own body, psyche, family, society and physical environment, as well as inter-generational effects. To us, reconstruction remains a crucial and effective technique for work with both closed- and open-system phenomena.

For more discussion and a detailed clinical example please see Novick, J. and Novick, K.K. 2015 "Working with "out-of-control" children – a two-systems approach"

[90] K.K. Novick and J. Novick 1987, and see the chapters on preschool and schoolage development in this volume

[91] J. Novick 1982b; J. Novick and K.K. Novick 2006

[92] J. Novick and K.K. Novick 1972

[93] Britton 2010, p.43

[94] Doidge 2007

[95] Rathbone 2001

[96] J. Novick and K.K. Novick 2001, 2006

[97] J. Novick and K.K. Novick 2000

[98] Lowenstein 1969

[99] E. Furman 1992

[100] See, for example, our 2012 review of Salberg

[101] J. Novick and K.K. Novick 2009

[102] R. Furman and E. Furman 1984

[103] J. Novick 1982; J. Novick and K.K. Novick 1996

[104] J. Novick and K.K. Novick 1996; K.K. Novick and J. Novick 1998; J. Novick and K.K. Novick 2006

[105] With small children, we talk about the "three buckets" – what children are in charge of, what grownups are in charge of, and what no one is in charge of. For more details, please see K.K. Novick and J. Novick "Emotional Muscle: Strong Parents, Strong Children" 2010.

[106] Burger et al 2013

[107] Kantrowitz 1997; Bergmann 1988

[108] Viorst 1982

[109] ibid.

[110] Sugarman 2015

[111] K.K. Novick et al 2001

[112] Homann 2013

[113] Feldman and Zaller 1992